T0343912

Travel guides?

EDITORIAL

47(02): 1/3 | DOI: 10.1177/0306422018785038

by **Rachael Jolley**

There are darker truths behind our favourite holiday destinations, but most people are unaware of them, writes **Rachael Jolley**

WHEN YOU READ a novel, it takes you on a journey to a different time or place. Being an avid reader of crime fiction, my early journeys to Chicago were in the company of Sara Paretsky. I walked the streets with her VI Warshawski. We shot down North Michigan Avenue and headed out to Wrigley Field for the fifth inning. Chicago opened up to me in those books – not always gloriously.

Donna Leon showed me around the small islands of the Venetian Lagoon and Ian Rankin has taken me on numerous tours of the dark closes of Edinburgh, as well as its swankier New Town.

Crime writers have less to lose than many other authors in describing the underside of the cities. After all, their readers don't expect a fairytale, and their escapism is a different kind from the happy-ever-afters of the perfect beach-read.

Perhaps we get more accurate portrayals of cities or countries by crime writers than in guidebooks or from travel apps.

Take Mexico and the Maldives, for instance. These are sexy holiday destinations, popular with everyone from honeymooners to scuba divers. But when thousands of holidaymakers are packing their sunscreen and swimsuits, do they know of the catastrophic numbers of journalists killed in Mexico in the past few years? Or how journalists in the Maldives are fleeing in fear of their lives?

Ad-hoc, non-scientific research, through the medium of asking friends and family, suggests not. And when that information is received, it is with some shock.

Mexico is ranked 147th out of 180 in the 2018 Reporters Without Borders World Press Freedom Index, down from 75th in 2002. During this period, tourist numbers have continued to go up. Meanwhile, 4.6% of the government's annual spend continues to go on tourism, significantly more than is spent in Brazil and New Zealand, for instance.

Travel and tourism delivers 6.9% of Mexico's GDP, compared with 3.3% of Brazil's and 5.1% of New Zealand's. No wonder, then, that Mexico's government is prepared to invest in tourism, and to keep that tap firmly switched on.

Informed tourists could be a powerful pressure point on governments that have been practising repression of those voices raised in criticism, or that don't bother to pursue the criminals who threaten or kill those voicing dissent.

At this year's Hay Festival, I was on a panel with Paul Caruana Galizia, son of the murdered journalist Daphne, as well as Malta journalist Caroline Muscat of The Shift News, and BBC Europe editor Katya Adler. Paul talked about his mother's work, the pressures she was under and how she pursued her investigations. We discussed the wider situation in Malta, where 34 libel cases against Daphne have, since her →

CREDIT: (top) Darrin Zammit Lupi/Reuters; Tyler Olson/Picfair

→ death, rolled over to the rest of the family. During the question and answer session, some members of the audience said they had no idea about what was going on in Malta, even though they went there on holiday, and asked what they could do to help.

Paul suggested that anyone holidaying on the Mediterranean island might mention being aware of the case to local people they met. The island was dependent on tourism, and if the Maltese felt this could be affected there would be more pressure on the government to alter its attitude, and legislation, on media freedom.

He also believed the Maltese government was much more worried about international attitudes than local ones.

In places where freedom of expression is under pressure – and Malta, the Maldives and Mexico are just a few of them – tourism is often a valuable asset. So visitors who are aware of the wider situation could be advocates for change.

According to analysis of travel, tourism, financial and freedom-of-expression data carried out for this magazine by Mark Frary, see p39, there are indications that some tourists want to know more than whether or not a destination has a good beach before they head off on holiday.

Data on travel patterns suggest that travellers also "reward" destinations that change legislation or the environment, his analysis suggests, with Argentina picking up significant tourist numbers after it became the first South American country to make gay marriage legal.

In this issue, we have asked reporters around the world to dig into the details of popular holiday destinations to look at their records on freedoms, such as the right to protest, the right to debate and freedom of the media. The results are stark. Many top tourism destinations do terribly on freedom of expression.

In post civil war Sri Lanka, there was a period of hope after the election of Prime

Minister Maithripala Sirisena in 2015. Many hoped that this beautiful island could have a future that was less violent, more equal and more open. Those hopes are now looking tarnished. As Meera Selva reports on p13, the country's tourist numbers grew spectacularly in 2017. But while tourists flocked in, the great improvement was not going as well as Sri Lankans had wished.

The prime minister has reactivated the Press Council – a body with the power to imprison journalists – and civil rights activists report threats against them. In this potential Eden, the garden is not as green and pleasant as predicted.

Pretty beach paradise Baja California Sur is a popular holiday destination, particularly for Americans. But not many will know that it also has the second-highest murder rate in Mexico, behind the western state of Colima, according to government data. The dangers of being an investigative journalist there are particularly high, with some living under 24-hour protection, as Stephen Woodman reports on p8. Again, this is a place where many (probably most) tourists are unaware of the fuller picture of the place where they are happily enjoying the sunshine.

As someone with a heritage collection of guidebooks from publishers including Lonely Planet, Rough Guides and Footprint, it is easy for me to flick through the pages and see that those guides have made a fair effort to inform readers on questions of human rights, politics and safety in the past.

But guidebooks are carried by far fewer travellers these days. According to the Financial Times, from 2005 to 2014, 9% fewer travellers left the UK but guidebook sales fell by 45%.

With most people looking to the web for all their holiday information, are they finding themselves as well-informed as they would have been with a well-thumbed book under their arm?

An April 2018 travel section article about Malta's capital Valletta on The Guardian's website doesn't mention the politics or human rights record of the island. Nor, as far as I could find, did the Lonely Planet website section on Malta. While, of course, it would be possible to find news about those issues on different parts of The Guardian site, or elsewhere on the web, it's certainly not connecting the dots for travellers.

With the printed travel sections of newspapers under pressure from advertisers – and far smaller than they were a decade ago – there is little space to create in-depth reports, and travel articles that include gritty details as well as the delights seem few and far between.

At the upcoming Index magazine launch and summer party on 4 July, our panel of experts will discuss what responsibility authors might have to tell their readers about the good, the bad and the ugly sides of any destination. It should be an interesting evening, chaired by BBC World reporter Vicky Baker, who also writes for Guardian Travel. If you would like to join us, email anna@indexoncensorship.org to grab a free ticket.

And since we are just back from the Hay Festival, we can also recommend our special Hay Festival podcast, where

Not many will know that it also has the second-highest murder rate in Mexico

deputy editor Jemimah Steinfeld chats to three authors about taboos. Catch it on Soundcloud.com/indexmagazine.

Finally, coming soon will be our regular quarterly magazine podcast, also on Soundcloud, including an interview with the founder of the Rough Guides, Mark Ellingham. Come by and visit us. ⊗

Rachael Jolley, editor, Index on Censorship

TWO SIDES OF VALLETTA, MALTA: (Opposite, top) Armed police officers of the Malta Police Special Intervention Unit provide security as three men, accused of the murder of Daphne Caruana Galizia, leave the courts of justice in Valletta in May 2018; (Opposite, below) an old, picturesque harbour in Valletta

CONTENTS

INDEX ON CENSORSHIP

VOLUME 47 NUMBER 02 – SUMMER 2018

CREDIT: Ben Jennings

BRITISH SOCIETY OF MAGAZINE EDITORS AWARDS 2016 WINNER

EDITOR
Rachael Jolley
DEPUTY EDITOR
Jemimah Steinfeld
SUB EDITORS
Tracey Bagshaw, Adam Aiken
CONTRIBUTING EDITORS:
Irene Caselli, Jan Fox (USA), Kaya Genç (Turkey), Laura Silvia Battaglia (Iraq and Yemen)

Index on Censorship | +44 (0) 20 7963 7262

292 Vauxhall Bridge Road, London SW1V 1AE, United Kingdom

EDITORIAL ASSISTANT
Danyaal Yasin
ART DIRECTOR
Matthew Hasteley
COVER
Ben Jennings
THANKS TO:
Jodie Ginsberg, Sean Gallagher, Ryan McChrystal

Magazine printed by Page Bros., Norwich, UK

Supported by
ARTS COUNCIL ENGLAND

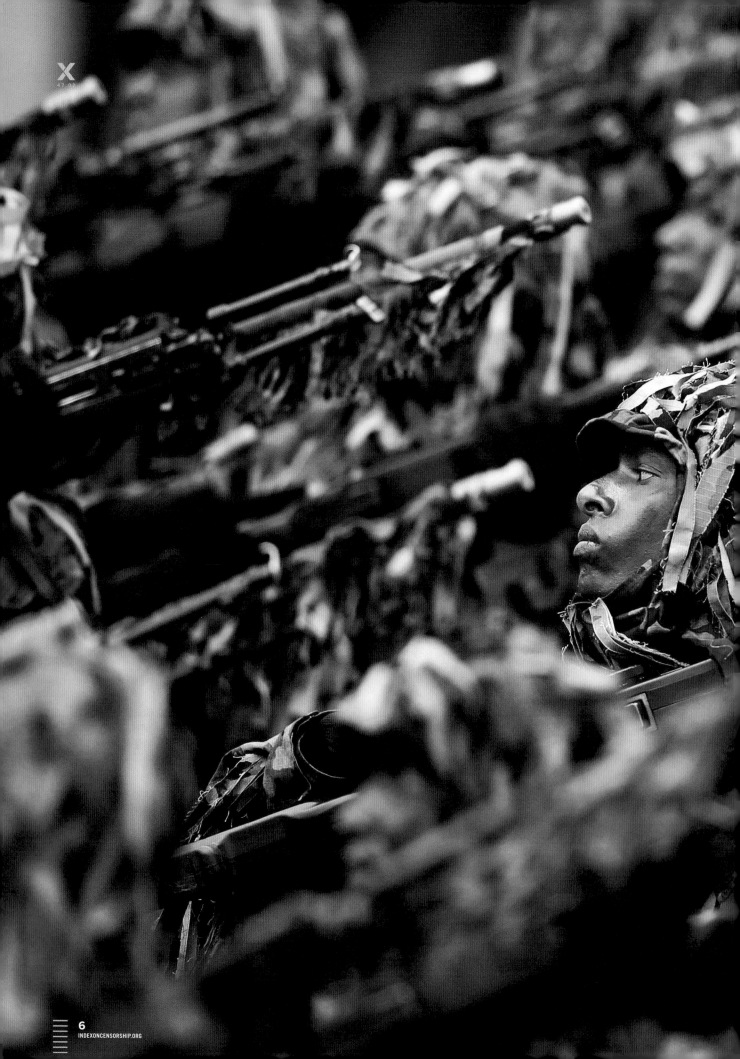

SPECIAL REPORT

TROUBLE IN PARADISE
ESCAPE FROM REALITY: WHAT HOLIDAYMAKERS
DON'T KNOW ABOUT THEIR DESTINATIONS

MAIN: Soldiers from the Sri Lankan army at a war victory parade in Colombo, 2012

CREDIT: Dinuka Liyanawatte/Reuters

Spraying bullets not sunscreen

47(02): 8/12 | DOI: 10.1177/0306422018784519

Tourists flock to beautiful Baja California Sur, but it is also at the forefront of Mexico's drug wars. The government doesn't want the holidaymakers to find out, writes **Stephen Woodman**

REPORTER JULIO OMAR Gomez has been suffering from severe anxiety since spring last year, when assailants shot his bodyguard outside his home in the northern Mexican state of Baja California Sur. After watching the guard die in hospital, Gomez realised he had no option but to leave his children and move to a location far from home.

Gomez, 38, is not the only journalist to have faced violence in Baja California Sur, a state which recently suffered a sudden spike in drug cartel-related crime. Although tourists still flock to its pristine beaches and high-end hotels, the destination has come to highlight the fragile state of the free press in Mexico – a country which celebrates its own Freedom of Expression Day on 7 June.

"The security profile of Baja California Sur has changed enormously, but because it's a tourist spot the government wants to hide that," Gomez told Index. "I told the stories of innocent victims and the mothers of sons who had disappeared. These articles tarnish the destination, but that's the reality."

Gomez is currently living in a safe-house provided under Mexico's Mechanism to Protect Human Rights Defenders and Journalists. Established in 2012, this programme offers panic buttons, bodyguards and safe-houses to media and human rights workers.

But Gomez has not found relief from his anxieties.

His protected status is up for review every six months, so he constantly worries about being removed from the programme. He also suspects a politician was behind the numerous attempts on his life and fears he will never be safe in Mexico.

After leaving Baja California Sur, Gomez battled suicidal thoughts and a mental health specialist put him on medication.

"Every day I feel a little less human, living on a cocktail of psychiatric drugs," Gomez said. "Surviving three attacks and then battling to survive day after day is not living at all. I want to live again."

Gomez became a target because of his website, 911 Noticias, which traced the gunfights and kidnappings that rocked the region.

Long regarded as a safe haven from drug violence, Baja California Sur hosts a tourist industry that has become the main pillar of its economy. The jewel in its crown is the municipality of Los Cabos – where Gomez lived and worked – which is currently Mexico's fourth most popular holiday spot for foreign visitors. At the southern-most point of the Baja California Peninsula, the municipality is a famed destination for whale-watching and fine-dining. Yet last year, there was an explosion of violence as competing criminal factions battled for control.

An edgy calm has returned since murders began to decline at the turn of the year, but the spike in violence still haunts the state. According to government data collected on Mexico's National Public Security System, the death toll rose from 192 in 2016 to 560 last year, giving Baja California Sur the second-highest murder rate in Mexico behind the western state of Colima.

Sheltered in the region's all-inclusive resorts, tourists have largely avoided the spiralling violence, although grisly scenes of bodies hanging from bridges and the fatal shooting of three men on a beach in Los Cabos last year have triggered alarm.

Conditions for journalists and human rights defenders also deteriorated as the drug war flared.

A fatal attack on the president of the state's human rights commission last November drew the condemnation of the United Nations. Assailants in the state capital, La Paz, fired into a car carrying Silvestre de la Toba Camacho, killing him and his son and injuring his wife and daughter.

Between 2009 and 2016, Article 19, the international press freedom campaign group, documented five acts of aggression against journalists in Baja California Sur.

By last year, that figure had soared to 16

OPPOSITE: Marijuana being incinerated at a military base in Tijuana, Baja California Sur, 2010. Drug cartel-related crime is currently on the rise

acts of aggression, including the murder of Gomez's mentor Maximino Rodríguez, a crime reporter who was shot dead in La Paz in April 2017.

Rodríguez was one of 11 Mexican journalists press freedom watchdog Reporters Without Borders says were murdered in connection with their work last year, putting Mexico ahead of Syria as the most dangerous country for reporters in the world.

The perpetrators have enjoyed complete impunity in 37 of the 45 killings monitored by the Committee to Protect Journalists since 1994.

Last May, in the face of rising national

Local outlets are dependent on government advertising to survive

and international criticism, Mexican President Enrique Peña Nieto promised to better protect the press. In June 2017, the government offered a reward of up to 1.5 million pesos ($78,769) for information on those responsible for attacks on several media workers, including Rodríguez.

In total, five suspects have been detained for their roles in the murder.

"One aspect that has not been →

clarified is who ordered the killing?" said Cuauhtémoc Morgan, the editor of Colectivo Pericu, the website which employed Rodríguez. "As an outlet we are still not satisfied."

However, Morgan welcomes the advances in the investigation and the state government's recent adoption of a more vocal stance on attacks against the press.

The motto "the right to the freedom of expression" was added to the wall of the state congress in June 2017.

After police aggression towards reporter Arturo Corona in the city Ciudad Constitución this April, state attorney general Daniel de la Rosa met him to offer support.

The attorney general's office did not respond to interview requests, but has previously declared in a statement that freedom

The death toll rose from 192 in 2016 to 560 last year, giving Baja California Sur the second-highest murder rate in Mexico

of expression was "a basic tenet of the administration".

Although this rhetoric is a welcome change, it stops a long way short of guaranteeing press safety.

In fact, authorities are the main culprit in attacks against the press in Mexico. Article 19 says public servants have been implicated in 48% of aggression against journalists since 2009.

"The government kills you if it can't silence you. That is their solution," said Rafael Silva, another reporter who fled the state for his life.

In November 2016, Silva, then 51, was standing at a petrol station in La Paz when he turned to see a man reaching for a gun. Shots rang out as he started to run and a passing bullet grazed his skull. Shaken and

bloodied, the reporter managed to escape by running into a house and clambering over the roofs of nearby buildings.

It was the third attempt on Silva's life in a campaign of terror that he blames on corrupt politicians with ties to organised crime.

"Many public officials are active, or have family members who are active, in drug trafficking organisations," Silva said. "Few journalists are willing to explore that."

Like Gomez, Silva is living under the government's protection outside of Baja California Sur. He laments the press freedom crisis that has gripped his home state.

"Journalists turn up at a crime scene and write about the event," he said. "They don't investigate who it was or what really happened."

According to Gladys Navarro, a reporter for El Universal newspaper, Rodríguez's murder fostered a climate of fear among reporters in the state, with coverage of cartel-related crimes coming to a standstill for several weeks.

She adds that media self-censorship also has economic roots. Few private companies spend much on advertising in Baja California Sur, so local outlets are dependent on government advertising to survive.

"Authorities take advantage of this situation," Navarro said. "They don't just buy advertising space, they buy the publication's editorial objectivity."

Navarro notes that independent websites such as Colectivo Pericú have forged a path for critical voices, despite the threatening environment behind the state's picture postcard image. She adds that attacks against journalists "violate society's right to inform itself" and threaten democracy.

"In Baja California Sur, we need to know when a hurricane is coming and what category it is," she said. "It's equally important that we are informed about the authorities." ⊗

Stephen Woodman is a journalist based in Guadalajara, Mexico

The other side of paradise

47(02): 13/16 I DOI: 10.1177/0306422018784532

The Sri Lankan government is drafting new laws to control social media this summer. In the 70th year since independence, Sri Lankans were hoping for a new liberal era, but **Meera Selva** reports on lack of progress

JAFFNA'S OLD PARK is where the new generation meet. The park, spacious and shaded, is where families come to let their children burn off some energy before bedtime and young women pose with their beaux for selfies and wedding photographs.

No one takes any notice of the fact that the blown-up remnants of a colonial era register office that was destroyed during the country's 26-year civil war are clearly visible nearby.

But the conflict, like the ruins, still casts a long shadow over Sri Lanka, and many fear hard-won freedoms are in retreat.

Women in this northern city, in particular, are acutely aware of what they have gained – and what they have lost – since the war ended in 2009. Many women joined the Tamil Tigers (LTTE) and fought with the same brutal efficiency as the men in the group's long battles against the Sri Lankan government. When the war ended, those who survived were sent to military-run "rehabilitation centres" where they were meant to receive vocational training to start a new life. In reality, they found themselves unskilled and ostracised by their communities.

"Once they strode about confidently. Today they have to go the extra mile to be as meek and mousy in the community as

possible to show that they have 'reformed'," said Thulasi Muttulingam, a journalist based in Jaffna.

"Apart from the various tabs kept on them by the government military, they are also under watch in their own communities and dare not step out of any demarcated boundaries."

More generally, women complain they feel intimidated by the high military presence and feel they are more vulnerable to sexual assault and rape than they were when the north was under the control of the LTTE, which had strict rules against sexual crimes.

Across the country, women who have gone into politics in response to recent electoral law reforms that stipulate 25% of all candidates must be women have been attacked by online trolls, religious groups and members of their own community.

Other groups are also feeling uneasy. President Maithripala Sirisena came to power in 2015, unseating the more authoritarian Mahinda Rajapaksa, who had drawn international condemnation for ordering the killing of civilians at the end of the civil war.

Sirisena won by calling Rajapaksa out on corruption, nepotism and the mismanagement of the economy, and by winning →

OPPOSITE: A Sri Lankan Muslim woman in Aluthgama in 2015, where Pope Francis visited to bring a message of peace between the Sinhalese majority and Tamil minority

→ the support of the country's Tamil and Muslim minorities.

He promised constitutional reform and transitional justice that was meant to bring perpetrators of war crimes to justice; to set up a system of reparations; and to open an office of missing persons to offer answers to the families of the thousands of civilians who had disappeared during the war.

The government also promised to investigate the killings of journalists, including the murder of Lasantha Wickrematunge, who was assassinated in 2009, just before he was due to give evidence in court against then-defence secretary Gotabaya Rajapaksa, the former president's brother.

The narrative was a powerful one, and in many ways it worked. Travel pages ran stories of new hotels and new tourists. The Sri Lankan Tourism Development Authority said the tourist arrivals to Sri Lanka reached an all-time high of 2.1 million in 2017.

Most visitors travel on a well-trodden

Six months after being elected, Sirisena re-activated the Press Council: a body that had the power to imprison journalists

circuit: covering Buddhist monuments in Kandy, Anuradhapura and Dambulla, alongside the ancient fortress of Sigiriya and the atmospheric ruined city of Polunaruwa before flopping on a beach.

The media, which had been so brutally supressed under Rajapaksa, began to breathe again. A huge variety of civil society groups stepped out from the shadows, calling for gay rights, women's empowerment and freedom of expression.

But the government has not repealed the Draconian Prevention of Terrorism Act that was long used by security forces to detain and torture suspects without charge, and

the outdated Penal Code, which criminalises same sex relations between adults, still holds.

And while the media is much freer than it was, journalists are still wary. Six months after being elected, Sirisena re-activated the Press Council: a body that had the power to imprison journalists.

Last year the investigative journalism website Groundviews found evidence that the president issued an order to block the news site Lanka E News.

Meanwhile, Prageeth Eknelygoda, a cartoonist and columnist for Lanka E News who was abducted in January 2010, is still missing.

The Committee to Protect Journalists said

CREDIT: Eranga Jayawardena/Rex

the authorities had not secured a single conviction in the cases of 10 Sri Lankan journalists murdered in retaliation for their work since 1992.

The investigation into Wickrematunge's assassination is still ongoing.

The result is a society where no one is clear what is acceptable and what is not.

Civil rights activists in the former war-torn areas of northern Sri Lanka report ongoing threats and intimidation from authorities.

Ruki Fernando, a civil rights activist who has been detained several times by authorities, says people still do not feel they have the full protection of the law.

"I recently got a call from Jaffna, where the family of a missing person has filed a court case against the authorities," he told Index. "Intelligence operatives had gone to these families to ask about the civil rights activists who had helped them bring the case to court. What is alarming is that this behaviour makes people afraid to bring cases to court.

"I don't think the top levels of government are ordering [the] mid-level to act like this, but they are sending out a strong signal that this behaviour is acceptable and there will be no punishment for it."

This feeling, that there is impunity for a certain section of society, intensified this →

→ year with a set of anti-Muslim riots that had echoes of the anti-Tamil pogroms of 1983 that pushed the country into war.

In February, at the tail end of Sri Lanka's peak holiday season, a group of Sinhala men went to eat at a Muslim restaurant in Ampara, some 45 miles inland from the trendy surfer hangout of Arugam Bay on the coun-

They are sending out a strong signal that this behaviour is acceptable and there will be no punishment for it

try's east coast. They spotted white powder on their plates and accused the owner of sprinkling powder that would render them infertile on their food.

Ethnic Sinhalese, who are predominantly Buddhist, make up 82% of the population, while Muslims make up just 8.5% but a certain strain of Sinhala nationalism has played on fears that the Sinhalese will be wiped out by the minority groups within their country.

The white powder turned out to be clumps of flour, but the rumours that Muslims were effectively trying to poison Sinhalese led to several Muslim-owned businesses and cars being attacked.

A few days later, a Sinhalese lorry driver was killed by four Muslim men near the town of Kandy: a town on Sri Lanka's tourist trail held as sacred by the country's majority Buddhist population. In retaliation, Sinhala mobs, encouraged by ultra-nationalist Buddhist monks, attacked mosques and businesses owned by Muslims.

CCTV footage of mosques that were attacked during the time, seen by the Reuters news agency, shows police officers hitting Muslim worshippers and clerics with batons.

The government declared a state of emergency for the first time since the end of the civil war, set up a curfew and placed a temporary ban on social media platforms including Facebook and WhatsApp, which it accused of encouraging the violence to spread.

The ban was lifted, and new regulations covering social media and hate speech are in the pipeline, but Sanjana Hattotuwa, the founder of Groundviews, says the focus on the role social media platforms played in spreading rumour and hate speech should not detract from the fact that much of the violence was implicitly or explicitly condoned by the government.

"Social media may have been an accelerant, but was not the cause of those riots. The larger, more visible and disturbing complicity is from the government that has done nothing to address the root causes of this anti-Muslim sentiment," he said.

There is a sense that the time for true reform is running out. The government is weak, reeling from party rifts and a disappointing performance in February's local elections. Rajapakse may well be able to come back to power, bringing back his authoritarian, Buddhist nationalist-dominated regime.

Many fear that the anti-Muslim riots are merely a precursor of what is to come. The government has not managed to protect minority rights nor hold anyone to account for their crimes. Authorities still collect information on activists and protesters.

The country still has wartime legislation that allows the government to suspend internet services, impose curfews and give police more powers to detain suspects without democratic scrutiny.

This, combined with a lack of progress in safeguarding freedom of association and in bringing high profile people to justice, means the country's new found freedoms can easily be snatched away. ⊗

Meera Selva is the director of the journalism fellowship programme at the Reuters Institute for the Study of Journalism, at the University of Oxford. Previously she was a journalist reporting on Nairobi, London, Berlin and Singapore

Speaking out of turn

47(02): 17/19 | DOI: 10.1177/0306422018784521

Just ahead of the Hawaiian public holiday honouring the historic kingdom, **Jan Fox** investigates how battles to keep the islands' native language alive are being thwarted at every turn

FOR MANY VISITORS, the Hawaiian Islands typify paradise. Tourists go to this Pacific Ocean state to swim and snorkel alongside turtles and dolphins in sparkling blue seas fringed by white sandy beaches and coral reefs. They explore lush rainforests, photograph dramatic waterfalls and enjoy spectacular sunsets.

Tales of an ancient culture that dates back hundreds of years will doubtless be part of the Kamehameha Day celebrations on 11 June, a public holiday honouring the native monarch who established the unified kingdom of Hawaii.

But beneath this beautiful exterior there are tensions. Hawaii is the only US state to have two official languages, yet they are far from equal – and the one that was there first gets the worst deal.

Forty years ago this year, Olelo Hawai'i (the native Hawaiian language) was officially incorporated into the state constitution as the state language, alongside English. It was seen as a great step forward considering that native Hawaiian had been banned by law as a medium of instruction since 1896. It was illegal to speak it in schools and pupils and teachers could be punished if caught doing so. It was also illegal for parents to speak native Hawaiian to their children in a public place, and it was even discouraged at home.

And while some progress has been made since 1978, there are still many restrictions on its use, notably in business, government and the courts, where English still rules.

Lawyer Camille Kalama, of the Native Hawaiian Legal Corporation, said: "Olelo Hawai'i is basically a second-class language."

In a court case on the island of Maui earlier this year, defendant Samuel Kaeo, wishing to testify in Hawaiian, was ignored by the judge despite the fact that Kaeo, a Hawaiian language advocate, was standing right in front of him, and the judge issued a warrant for Kaeo's arrest for not showing up in court.

Kalama said: "I was in shock. This was a blatant example of a judge not even acknowledging someone's physical presence, just because they chose to speak in Hawaiian. The judge treated Mr Kaeo as if he were invisible."

"It's our right. Why shouldn't we be able to speak Hawaiian when it's a state language? What does that mean if we can't defend ourselves? It means if we speak in English we exist, but if we speak in Hawaiian we don't. It's a punishment for speaking our own language."

In this particular case, said Kalama, the defendant was known to the judge. Kaeo, a frequent public protester for native rights, had come before him on another occasion.

"Mr Kaeo had already shown up three times for this case (travelling from another island) and was told no translator was →

ABOVE: Traditional Hawaiian ceremony to mark the opening of the 2015 Target Maui Pro at Honolua Bay, Maui, Hawaii

→ available. So his choice ends up being, do I speak English, or do I maintain my right to speak Hawaiian?" said Kalama.

"There are things that can be expressed differently in our language and that a defendant needs access to when trying to explain why they did something. Legal terms are also often difficult to translate."

The inability to speak Hawaiian in court is symptomatic of a wider problem, says Kalama.

"We are constantly forced to speak English and that's a hindrance to full fluency in Hawaiian and keeping the language truly alive. Mr Kaeo's court case showed the attitude we see all too often that if you can speak English then you should. It just showed how far we have to go."

Another issue Kalama's office is dealing with is the right of prisoners to receive letters in Hawaiian. She explains that Hawaii has run out of prison space and contracts out to prisons in Arizona.

"We had a case where an inmate received a letter in Hawaiian, but the prison refused to accept it because they had no one to translate it into English, yet they have translators for many other languages, including Polynesian and Micronesian ones, so it's just another excuse," said Kalama. At the time of going to print, this case was in the circuit court of the US justice system and was as yet unresolved.

"Within the prison system, Hawaiian cultural and religious practice is also looked on as a privilege and not a right," said Kalama. "People ask why we have to push for the right to express ourselves here on our own islands and I think for many colonised peoples there's a hesitancy to push, but my children's generation are more likely to say: 'Why am I learning Hawaiian if I can't use it?' and that's hopeful.

"We are currently suing the state on the island of Lanai for failure to provide a Hawaiian language school because there are waiting lists and kids can't get in. If we want to preserve Hawaiian as a living language, it needs to be used more in daily life, and government needs to do more to make this happen."

Puakea Nogelmeier, professor of Hawaiian

language at the University of Hawaii, said: "In courts, people have started to demand the right to speak it, but the state's attitude is very much one of, why should we pay interpreters? It's a luxury and if people can speak English then they should. But that's what equality is supposed to be about – the right to choose from two official languages."

After the Kaeo case, the state judiciary promised to look at supplying more interpreters "to the extent reasonably possible" but it's unclear what that will mean.

"I'm hopeful this has called attention to the problem but I think the state has its own agenda," said Nogelmeier. "We already have a certification programme for interpreters for other languages on the island, such as Japanese, Korean, Polynesian languages, but Hawaiian has no certification at all. This means translators are selected by level and we just hope these people have enough expertise to do the job. These translators are also paid below the level of certified translators."

He added: "Originally, the kingdom of Hawaii was multi-racial but Hawaiian was the official language. It's the natural language but now it's just a hobby in the eyes of some people and that's patronising, too."

Repression has a long history here. The kingdom of Hawaii was overthrown in 1893 and formally annexed by the USA in 1898, although Nogelmeier points out that, as there was never any formal treaty, the Hawaiian sovereignty movement claim the islands are illegally occupied. It became the 50th state in 1959.

After being banned, Hawaiian was driven underground, gradually native speakers died off and by the early 1970s, said Nogelmeier, there were fewer than 1,000 people who could speak it. A grassroots movement from parents led to the state introducing immersion schools, where pupils study only in Hawaiian until they reach fifth grade. Testing has still been in English, however, which caused controversy because it disadvantaged pupils.

"Around 25,000 people can now speak Hawaiian at varying levels so they have the ability, but when they leave college there is little to no opportunity to use it outside the home. It's a huge restraint on expression. I do believe in part that there's an inherent American suspicion of bilingualism that's held by a certain proportion of the population – it's become an aspect of American culture," said Nogelmeier.

Due to retire this month, Nogelmeier will continue to work with the non-profit To Bind Together In Unity, mentoring translators and helping them explore massive written archives left by their ancestors which few people are now able to read.

But he hopes that, through the passion of young people, this will change. "I hope Hawaiian will be spoken more widely by the community in the 22nd century, but I can't see it happening before then," he said.

Also hopeful of change is 34-year-old Kendall Kanoa Kukahiko, descendant of an honoured *kumu hula* (hula master) who teaches hula in Los Angeles.

She says hula is much more than a dance performed for tourists.

If we speak in English we exist, but if we speak in Hawaiian we don't

"It's woven into every part of Hawaiian life and culture, and when the language was driven underground it was a way to still tell our stories through dance and chants. Unfortunately, it's a form of expression that's been appropriated by many people who teach it at a superficial level and it's not taken very seriously by some, but it helps keep our language alive. We see ourselves as the keepers of the language." ⊗

Jan Fox is a contributing editor for Index on Censorship, based in Los Angeles

Women left out in the cold

47(02): 20/22 | DOI: 10.1177/0306422018784523

Bali is known as much for its warm people as its beautiful beaches.
But this reputation hides issues of domestic violence, writes
Johannes Nugroho

EACH YEAR, MILLIONS of people flock to the tropical beach paradise that is Bali. While arguably more scenic and exotic destinations exist elsewhere within the Indonesian archipelago, Bali bests the others in one inimitable asset: the reputation of its people as being hospitable. This reputation is partly fed by an assumption that the mainly Hindu Balinese are relatively liberal compared with those in the mostly Muslim parts of Indonesia. Balinese women traditionally went about their business bare-breasted until the 1950s when President Sukarno put a stop to the practice in the name of nationalism.

But these seemingly modern attitudes have their limits. For Bali's women, a strong patriarchal society means many are without

CREDIT: Sonny Tumbelaka/Afp/Getty

a voice. This reality was seen in horrific fashion at the end of last year when a local woman, Ni Putu Kariani, had her legs mutilated by her jealous husband. The husband had been abusive for years and yet whenever she told her parents, they simply asked her to "have patience".

In this instance, the man was recently sentenced to eight years in prison although, according to the court transcript, his wife appears to have lost custody of her child to her mother-in-law. For other women, justice – if it can be called that – has not been served. In 2017 alone, 118 cases of domestic violence were reported in Bali, according to local news site Bali Ekbis. It is believed most victims never step forward and domestic abuse remains a problem.

While the Kariani news story raced around the Indonesian media and was published on the BBC's Indonesia site in Indonesian, it never made it into major international media. With the exception of the terrorist attacks back in 2002, Bali's reputation as a paradise remains. And so, too, does the patriarchy.

Although the earliest Balinese women's rights movement dates back to the 1930s, with the founding of organisations such as Putri Bali Sadar, there have been few changes to the rules and taboos governing the island's population, known as *hukum adat*, which remain vigorously patriarchal.

Inheritance customs are another example of the difficulties women face. Traditionally barred from inheriting from their husbands or parents until a 2010 ruling said they had the same rights to inherit as men, women continue to be left out. Kadek Wirawan, a Balinese history expert from Denpasar, the island's capital, points out that most Balinese still practise male primogeniture in matters of inheritance.

"By customary law, women can only inherit if her status as *pradhana* (feminine) is changed to *purusha* (masculine). Families with no male heir usually adopt this practice.

Women whose status is *purusha*, however, can't be proposed to – they have to propose to their prospective husbands!"

Komang Triyani, a working mother from Tabanan in central Bali, admits that her culture strongly favours the male, but argues that it is not without reason.

"It is also men who have to continue the family line, carry out religious rituals for the ancestors and so on," she said. "This is why most Balinese consider having a son to be extremely important. As a Balinese, I can accept this."

Triyani's ready acceptance of the status quo appears to be common among Balinese women. When conducting interviews for this article, the overwhelming majority of respondents were reluctant to share their views on gender equality – it appeared to be a taboo topic. Most who were willing to speak defended the paternalistic customs and tended to see it as something that was somehow immutable.

But some are critical. Luh Manis, an entrepreneur and trained Jero (a Balinese priestess), says that even though she loves the Balinese culture, she takes issue with the lack of equality.

Those who dare criticise our own customs must be prepared to face ostracism by their neighbours

"There's definitely a taboo on women speaking about our customary laws, which are seen to be the domain of men," she said. "Customary-laws councils, even at the lowest village level, are dominated by men, which is why the rules tend to disregard women's needs."

The inability of women to speak about inequality looks set to continue. Bali has its regional election on 27 June and none of the candidates are female. →

OPPOSITE:
Balinese women take part in a Melasti ceremony in Kuta, a resort in the south of the island

→ Wayan Jarrah Sastrawan, a PhD student of Asian history at the University of Sydney, argues that *hukum adat* should move with the times.

"Many Balinese people don't have a strong sense for the history of their *adat* law, but basically see [it] as fixed or at least very difficult to change, despite the fact that *adat* law has always been dynamic and responsive to change," he said.

Sastrawan, who has studied Sanskrit and ancient Balinese, believes that gender inequality in Bali has ancient roots.

"The scriptural base of Balinese religion is a set of Hindu documents (some in Sanskrit, most translated into Kawi and Balinese) that are very misogynistic."

The combination of treating *hukum adat* as being set in stone and pervasive misogyny

The drive to preserve their hereditary customs often takes precedence over gender equality

has resulted in self-censorship among Balinese women.

"Those who dare criticise our own customs must be prepared to face ostracism by their neighbours and even family members," Manis said. "This is true especially in small villages where social conformity is high. At the very least, you'll be the talk of the village."

Since most Balinese are raised to attach great importance to religious rites of passage, an existence cut off from society is unthinkable. While there are civil society organisations advocating women's emancipation in Bali, most toe the line when it comes to "respecting" customary law. The few exceptions that remain critical tend to receive minimal support from both society and government.

Feminist magazine Bali Sruti blazed a trail for seven years. Under an NGO with the same name, it consistently took to task various forms of discrimination towards women and was often critical of the patriarchal elements in Balinese society. But it had to cease publication last year due to lack of funding.

With added pressure on the Balinese as a minority culture within Muslim-majority Indonesia, the drive to preserve their hereditary customs often takes precedence over gender equality, making it difficult to tolerate critical thoughts from outsiders, let alone self-criticism.

The future of advocacy for women's rights on the island seems to depend on the initiative of its women to express themselves more freely.

"I think it's important for women in Bali to speak out. Not enough of us do – even our most accomplished women shy away from being frank, out of deference for our customs," Manis said.

With these strong traditions and another set of men due to be the leaders of Bali from the end of June, how – and when – will women gain a voice? ⊗

Johannes Nugroho is a writer based in Surabaya, East Java in Indonesia. He has just finished his first novel on the hidden history of ancient matriarchal Java

Rocking the nation

47(02): 23/25 I DOI: 10.1177/0306422018784524

Malaysia is far from a multi-ethnic paradise, as its musicians will tell you. Will anything change with the new governmnent, asks **Marco Ferrarese**

THE DAY AFTER Malaysia's 14th general election, on 10 May 2018, the air was filled with an indescribable feeling of hope. The National Front, led by exiting Prime Minister Najib Razak, had eaten into the country's social and political sphere like a throat cancer, suffocating the freedom of expression of multi-ethnic Malaysians of all ages, creeds and classes. And now they had been unexpectedly voted out.

The National Front, a predominantly ethnic-Malay party, has run Malaysia since its formation in 1957, the longest time a political coalition has ever held power in the world. Compared with Malaysia's other ethnic groups, the Malays hold special native rights (the *bumiputera* status) which, for example, give them favoured treatment in terms of access to higher education, work placements and the ability to buy housing. Their religion, Islam, has been used as a normative tool to justify their social and political decisions. It has been hard for other ethnic groups to have a voice.

And yet this is not the image the government has been portraying. Landing in Kuala Lumpur, visitors are confronted with leaflets that promote "Malaysia, Truly Asia", a paradise land of beautiful white-powder beaches, transparent seas and endless rainforests, where three of Asia's main ethnic groups — the Chinese, the Indians and the Malays — peacefully co-exist. In the city proper, the National Front's propaganda hasn't even spared the Light Rapid Transport network: information screens are often filled with another fickle, beautifying, multi-ethnic campaign, 1Malaysia.

The government has tried to broadcast the convincing image of a united, harmonious, multi-ethnic nation. And it has poured lots of money into tourism (projects to improve infrastructure in Langkawi, for example, were recently announced). These efforts work, to an extent; millions of tourists flock to Malaysia's capital and beaches each year.

Speaking out against this lie can get you in trouble. But not all are willing to remain silent, and amongst the most outspoken are Malaysia's underground musicians. In this nation where mainstream media has been tightly controlled by the National Front, underground music scenes have provided a space where young Malaysians can voice their real opinions.

Take Kuala Lumpur's melodic punk band Dum Dum Tak, well-known on the scene for their outspoken and daring lyrics. They play in underground venues such as rented halls and rehearsal studios, which are hard to access for general tourists who rarely explore beyond Malaysia's famous tourist hotspots.

Ahmad Nizammudin, the band's bass player, backing vocalist and main lyricist, said they sang "about dirty politics [and] the dictatorship of the ruling party". They have a song bashing Razak and the 1Malaysia Development Berhad scandal, which saw →

RIGHT: Anti-fascist skinhead punk band Street Boundaries performs at Soundmaker, a long-standing alternative music venue and studio on the island of Penang

→ state funds equivalent to $700m allegedly siphoned off to his personal accounts, and they sing about the goods and services tax – "a tax applied to everyone, including the poor".

"Other bands sing about these topics, but the fact our songs are melodic and in Malay [means we] attract even people outside the punk-rock scene," he said.

Not all are willing to remain silent, and amongst the most outspoken are Malaysia's underground musicians

"We try to organise events and produce music that allow or encourage people to be critical towards society and the media," said Cole Yew, a Malaysian Chinese guitarist of multi-ethnic "stoner rock" band White Crow and manager of Soundmaker, northern Malaysia's prominent independent music venue and studio, which is located on the tourist island of Penang.

"It's a way of practising our rights: artists should be more socially aware in order to maintain a healthy music and art movement that supports constructive social values."

Malaysia's underground music scene stretches back to the mid-1980s, when Anglo-American music and magazines such as NME reached the country and spawned heavy metal and punk bands. Blackfire, a metal band formed in 1982 in the state of Perlis, is believed to be Malaysia's first heavy-rock outfit.

The positive, egalitarian themes promoted by global underground sub-cultures helped give young Malaysians an alternative. By the late 1990s, Kuala Lumpur's Central Market had become the meeting place and breeding ground for a number of young, multi-ethnic Malaysian artists and musicians, who were disillusioned with the increasingly conservative mindset of the rural Malay hinterland.

These first bands enjoyed the tail end of musical freedom in Malaysia which, throughout the 1980s, saw long-haired, scruffy "mat rockers" (Malay hard rock fans and musicians) such as Search, Wings and Kembara obtain popular success. They recorded platinum albums and packed Kuala Lumpur's stadiums to the gills, playing a mix of melodic European hard rock and lyrics sung in the Malay language that appealed to all races and segments of society.

The government initially paired with the mat rockers to promote Malaysia – see Cinta Buatan Malaysia (Love Made in Malaysia), Search's 1985 debut album, and a song of the same name that promoted local industry. But a few years later, the loud voice of hard music ended up being curbed by the hardest Islamic line in the political sphere: during the Mahathir era in 2001 and 2006, authorities cracked down on an alleged rise in "Satanic black metal fans" who "fornicated freely and desecrated the Koran". As a result, the whole music scene was shot down in flames: records were confiscated, shows were cancelled and the events were sensationalised by the Malay-language media.

"It was a classic case of societal 'moral panic' created, and further inflamed, by the always opportunistic, moral-baiting media," said Joe Kidd, ethnic-Malay guitarist of Carburetor Dung, one of Malaysia's pioneering punk bands, and an authority in the local scene.

"The local metal scene was old and mature enough to know that it was a seasonal occurrence. They just laid low for a few months, waited for the heat to dissipate, and then sprang back into action, like countless of times before since the beginning of the scene in the late '80s."

Today, performers and organisers have learnt to maintain low profiles. When political cartoonist and punk activist Fahmi Reza – who was recently sentenced for "violating

multi-media laws" with his famous caricature of Razak as an evil-looking clown – posted Dum Dum Tak's song Turun Najib Turun (Get Down, Najib, Get Down) to his online following in 2016, the band refused a resulting interview request from the BBC.

"We thought about the risks, and realised we have commitments towards our families as breadwinners, so we declined," explained Nizammudin, who feared repercussions.

Azmyl Yunor, a songwriter, singer of multi-ethnic punk band Ben's Bitches and a senior lecturer at the department of performance and media of Sunway University, near Kuala Lumpur, said Malaysian musicians and songwriters "self-regulate on what they deem to be 'safe' or 'unsafe' expressions".

When Yew was interviewed, he was about

The government has tried to broadcast the convincing image of a united, harmonious, multi-ethnic nation

to return to his home town of Brinchang in the Cameron Highlands to vote, hoping for a new and more open-minded government. With this crucial election result, perhaps his wish has been granted and the country might more closely resemble the Malaysia of the tourist brochures. ⊗

Marco Ferrarese is an author and freelance journalist based in Malaysia. He has co-authored guidebooks on the country for Rough Guides

47(02): 26/27 | DOI: 10.1177/0306422018784525

Rowson

MARTIN
ROWSON is a
cartoonist for
The Guardian
and the author
of various books,
including The
Communist Man-
ifesto (2018),
a graphic novel
adaption of the
famous 19th
century book

Two sides of every story

47(02): 28/31 I DOI: 10.1177/0306422018784526

We speak to two leading authors, **Victoria Hislop** and **Ian Rankin**, about why it has been important for them to talk about the taboos and undersides of top tourist destinations

THE FULL STORY

VICTORIA HISLOP talks to ALISON FLOOD about the role of a country's gritty history in her "summer beach reads"

For a long time, says novelist Victoria Hislop, her best-seller The Island came emblazoned with a reviewer's quote on the cover: "a beach book with a heart". This was, in a way, true – the novel is set on the Greek island of Spinalonga, but is far from a slice of holiday romance in a sunny Greek paradise. The Island delves into the history of the location, revealing its brutal past as a former leper colony.

"It was definitely read a lot on the beaches that summer, and at the heart of the book was a very tough reality – a story of a once-incurable disease," said Hislop, who is now an ambassador for leprosy charity Lepra.

"It's fine for people to go to the Greek islands and lie on a beach with a beer in their hand. I would never want to stop them. Greece is paradise, in its way. But at the same time, the 20th century was a very dark time – full of conflict, war, poverty – and I suppose my point is that these dark periods explain why Greece is as it is now. And that's what I explore."

Hislop was moved to write The Island, her debut novel, after a visit to the former leper colony.

"Without doubt there was a stigma surrounding it – and something buried [or] hidden acts like a magnet for a writer. This isn't a criticism of the Greeks per se. Unlike most diseases, leprosy in general has a stigma attached to it (Leviticus suggests that it is a punishment from God, and that sufferers should be shunned), so locally, the story of this island had not been promoted very broadly because people were ashamed of it," she said.

"Some of these islands that people go to for peace and paradise were once used as islands of exile (in the 1940s and 50s, some in the 60s) for thousands of people who had fought for the Left. The locals might not tell them that, but I will, because it's interesting and should not be forgotten, in my view. They

CREDIT: (left) Ioanna Tzetzoumi; Alexander Chaikin/Pictair

RIGHT: Victoria Hislop writes beach reads with "heart", but also honesty

ABOVE: The beach in Ayia Napa, Cyprus, an island which has seen unrest and violence in recent decades

were imprisoned for their views, some for years and deprived of their human rights."

Published in 2005, The Island was picked for the Richard and Judy Book Club, and went on to sell a million copies. Hislop's subsequent novel, The Return, was set in Granada, looking into its violent past; The Thread centres on Thessaloniki; and The Sunrise on Cyprus.

"Wherever people go to relax and get away from it all, there is probably a darkness lurking nearby," Hislop said. "Spain is another example, which was why I wrote The Return. I had been lying on a beach in a bikini in the 1970s without any idea that there were still people in prison, probably not far away, simply for being on the 'wrong' side in their civil war back in the 1930s. Franco had crushed the opposition so heavily that we Brits were lapping up the sunshine oblivious of his crimes. I suppose I felt guilty about that in retrospect – and wish I had known. The truth about what happened during the Spanish Civil War (and the repression afterwards) would definitely have been a good thing for the average tourist to know."

Her readers – holidaymakers or otherwise – have certainly been keen to explore the darker side of paradise that Hislop portrays. But covering the Cyprus conflict in The Sunrise led to the loss of some of her Greek readers.

"There were some Greek Cypriots who were angry that I had implied that the Turkish invasion of Cyprus was provoked by a Greek army coup in the country. And not only that, some of my most sympathetic characters were Turkish Cypriots – and the villain was a Greek Cypriot," she said. "My point was that being a good [or] bad human being is not a matter of ethnicity. It is more than that."

According to Hislop, fiction is "a really valid way to tell a story which explores the truth of a country's history".

"Of course 'truth' is often a matter of opinion and its definition is fought over by historians – so I am very conscious of the responsibility not to be biased in one or other direction if there is any ambiguity. This, of course, is done by having the characters taking different points of view, and then you almost hand it over to the reader to decide (whilst knowing yourself where you stand)," she said.

Alison Flood *is a freelance journalist, The Guardian's books reporter and former news editor of The Bookseller*

BEYOND THE BAGPIPES

The king of "tartan noir", IAN RANKIN, tells JEMIMAH STEINFELD about exposing parts of Edinburgh the tourists don't see

Ian Rankin writes crime fiction because, for him, it's one of the best ways to accurately depict somewhere and not censor out the less palatable sides.

"The reason I turned to crime fiction is I think it's the perfect way to scratch the surface of a place, of a culture, of a country, of a society, and show what's underneath, the good and the bad," he told Index. "So if you want to talk about social issues, if you want to talk about political corruption, and if you want to talk about corruption in business, immigration policy, xenophobia, all of that, you can deal with a police officer who is looking for the truth."

The best-selling novelist explains that when it came to Edinburgh, the setting of his Inspector Rebus series, showing the city in its various shapes and guises wasn't typical at the time he started writing. He first arrived in Edinburgh as a student in the late 1970s, and from then to the early 1980s, the city had a lot of issues.

"It had problems with drugs, it had problems with unemployment and social problems, problems with prostitution. And yet, you know, I would watch the tourists come and go and of course they got no sense that this city had any problems like that at all. They were just happy to see the castle and they would see someone play the bagpipes and they would go to the museum and think they had seen Edinburgh and, of course, they had only really seen the one side of it."

Rankin says Robert Louis Stevenson's portrayal of the different sides of Edinburgh in his 1886 book The Strange Case of Dr Jekyll and Mr Hyde was a notable influence, but adds that the literature of the late 20th century was avoiding the city's harder truths.

"In literature, in the novel, not much had been done with Edinburgh since The Prime of Miss Jean Brodie, you know [Muriel] Spark's novel, which had been written in 1961 and was set in the 1930s. So I thought 'if nobody's writing about contemporary Edinburgh, I'd like to give it a go'. And then, you know, shortly afterwards along came Trainspotting and showed the wider world, courtesy of the movie, that there is more to Edinburgh than the castle and the tartan and the bagpipes."

RIGHT: Ian Rankin, whose Rebus series shows Edinburgh's good and bad sides

ABOVE: Two aspects of Edinburgh – the beautiful one the tourists see (right) and its edgier other persona, as depicted in the film Trainspotting

Equally, crime writers have to ensure they don't go too dark in their portrayal of a place and miss the nuance for the opposite reason.

"It's getting slightly frustrating for me when I write about my character Rebus because he is a professional cynic," said Rankin.

"He's been in the job so long that he cannot see the other side of Edinburgh. He cannot see the Jekyll, he only sees it as the Hyde, he only sees it as crime scenes that have happened, or crime scenes that might happen in the future, so other characters have to be roped in to show him that he does live in a very beautiful city, a very literary city and a very cultured city."

When not in Edinburgh, Rankin spends time in a small, seemingly idyllic fishing village in northern Scotland called Cromarty, which he is tempted to airbrush.

"When I post photographs of it on social media, I'm always careful to point the camera one way because if you point it the other way all you see are oil rigs and an oil rig yard. So there's industry up there, it's not the kind of tartan, shortbread image of Scotland.

"But it's a lovely, small town on the coast where there are dolphins playing and everybody knows everybody," he added.

Rankin understands why visitors might only want to see one side. "Tourists to any city in the world will tend to go to the attractions and the attractions are usually the nice things," he said.

Speaking specifically of when he's on a book tour, he said: "You tend to see the nice places, you tend to stay in quite nice hotels, you get taxis everywhere, people take you out for meals and you go to bookshops and radio stations and TV studios. You don't tend to go to the ghettos, you don't tend to go to the rougher parts of town because there are no bookshops there, so why would you?"

Asked where Rankin has personally observed a big gap between the tourist brochures and reality, he replies, with little hesitation – India.

"I shouldn't have been surprised by India, but I still was," he said. He spoke of taking a train through Delhi first thing in the morning and seeing "people brushing their teeth by the railway tracks, defecating by the railway tracks, eating a breakfast by the railway tracks, having slept out by the railway tracks".

He added: "You've got this country which is seething with colour and life and vitality and culture and history, but also has huge, huge problems and they're visible, they're visible to the visitor, and I wasn't quite expecting that."

Jemimah Steinfeld *is deputy editor of Index*

CREDIT: Darrin Zammit Lupi/Reuters

Double vision

47(02): 32/34 | DOI: 10.1177/0306422018784527

Malta's beautiful tourist image masks a murky underside of this
Mediterranean island, writes **Caroline Muscat**

THE SPRAWL OF construction sites repre-
sents the reality of Malta. It's a sign of
progress, never mind the fact that planning
laws are farcical. The country's affluence is
shown by the number of cars on the road,
never mind the traffic congestion. Its freedom is evidenced in the number of media
outlets and news portals, never mind the
fact that they all offer similar content. It's
all about appearance, not substance. Scratch

beneath the surface and the problems start
to appear.

"National pride has reached historic
levels," Prime Minister Joseph Muscat told
more than 100,000 people who flocked to
the nation's capital, Valletta, for its inauguration as Europe's Capital of Culture 2018.
The announcement was made as the country
was grappling with the assassination of its
most prominent journalist, Daphne Caruana

The links date back to 1974, when a Sicilian man and his bride went to the Maltese island of Gozo on their honeymoon. They loved the island so much they frequently returned. To the locals who interacted with him in Pjazza San Frangisk, in Victoria, he was known simply as Toto.

But Toto was Salvatore Riina, the mafia boss who terrorised Sicily and made the Italian State tremble while making friends in Malta.

Over the years, Malta has continued to attract shady characters, including politically exposed politicians, from countries including India, Ukraine and Azerbaijan. There are clear risks in probing too deeply into the shadows of modern Malta – not that this is obvious to anyone landing in the country for a fortnight of sun and sea. Popular events, such as the annual music festival the Isle of MTV, continue to offer a distraction on the islands that were once a safe haven for tourists and locals. But the recent release of the Panama Papers linked a Maltese minister, Konrad Mizzi, and the prime minister's chief of staff, Keith Schembri, to $1.6m payments to Dubai companies. Both deny the claims of payments.

LEFT: A demonstrator carries a photo of assassinated anti-corruption journalist Daphne Caruana Galizia during a protest against government corruption in Valletta, Malta, April 2018

Galizia, and as accusations of a collapse in the rule of law continued to haunt Malta.

Restaurants offering mouth-watering dishes are found across the length and breadth of Malta's islands, but while digging into a bruschetta few stop to question the sudden influx of Sicilian restaurants that are suspected of being money-laundering fronts for the Sicilian mafia.

Operation Beta, led by the Italian authorities in 2017, culminated in the arrest of 30 people as part of a major clampdown on illegal gaming activities and money laundering linked to a Sicilian family, the Santapaola-Erculanos, linked to the mafia by the Italian media. Almost a year later, Italian police cracked an operation involving Sicilians, Maltese and Libyans smuggling Libyan fuel into the European market. Once again, a link to the Santapaola-Erculano family emerged. A look at the histories of the mafia clans reveals deep family connections to Malta as a hub from which to extend their reach and profits.

Few stop to question the sudden influx of Sicilian restaurants that are suspected to be money-laundering fronts

It is now clear that a political party elected in 2013 on the promise of change was not thinking of adding transparency or media freedom. Since the Panama Papers revelations, journalists have piled up stories of scandals, but nothing has changed. Deals selling off the country's assets continue to be made, shrouded in secrecy. And in the midst of all this, calls for justice for an assassinated journalist continue to echo in the air. →

→ Daphne Caruana Galizia was killed because of what she exposed. Seven months later, the institutions that failed to protect her are the same institutions that are failing to bring those who ordered her killing to justice. Every month, on the date marking her death, citizens gather to call for justice in the country's capital. They gather in front of a makeshift memorial before the law courts as a reminder that justice has not been served. Every time, they know they will see each other the following month because nothing will have changed. Yet their presence, and the flowers and candles placed at the foot of the monument, serve as a reminder to the authorities that they will never forget.

Those who mention her name, those who refuse to bow to a society bent by corrup-

But the Paradise Papers had already shown just how "fantastic" Malta was by casting a dark cloud over its economic miracle

tion, are insulted and threatened. Journalists and activists keep being reminded of the untold damage they are doing to the country's reputation. Malta's image is everything, but it is not what it seems.

When confronted by the news that the European Parliament was sending a delegation to investigate Malta's anti-money laundering rules, Muscat said: "I invite them to come over to see what a fantastic country we are." But the Paradise Papers had already shown just how "fantastic" Malta s by casting a dark cloud over its economic miracle.

While workers in other countries have borne the brunt of austerity, the Maltese have never had it so good, shielded by an economic system which relies partly on enticing shell companies to Malta by offering a favourable fiscal regime, in addition to a growing dependence on i-gaming and construction. In addition, Malta's controversial "sale" of European passports continues, despite concerns about the erosion of democracy.

Living in Malta as a journalist one experiences the stark reality of it all. Those exposing corruption are ostracised and vilified. Their voices are drowned out by the millions spent on the marketing machine to promote Malta and clean its image. Journalism is undermined through an almost complete domination of the narrative by the government – millions of euros spent on PR ridicules weeks of investigative journalism. Government advertising drowns out calls for a democracy that ends corruption and protects freedom of speech.

On 16 May, Labour MP Rosianne Cutajar stood up in parliament and spent 30 minutes criticising the publication of a six-month investigation by The Shift News that exposed pro-government secret Facebook groups with thousands of members posting threats against activists. These posts included threats towards anti-corruption activist Tina Urso, whose home address was also published on the site. Urso filed two complaints with the police, but wasn't offered any protection.

The MP also said I was sowing the seeds of hatred left behind by Caruana Galizia by attacking the government. Compare this with the exposé of anti-Semitism in the UK Labour Party and the media scandal that followed. In Malta, the scandal was the journalist who dared to speak truth to power.

Caruana Galizia had written: "Malta is in a dangerous place, and now we can no longer say that it is corrupt politicians who have brought it to this point, for it can no longer be denied that those corrupt politicians are a reflection of society."

In this scenario, the protection of journalists is critical in a landscape that is intolerant of independent thought. ⊗

Caroline Muscat is the co-founder of The Shift News, based in Malta

Taking on the untouchables

47(02): 35/38 I DOI: 10.1177/0306422018784528

The picturesque seaside town of Ostia has escaped the mafia reputation of Sicily, but not the mafia itself. **Irene Caselli** talks to crime reporter **Federica Angeli** about living with 24-hour protection and worries the new Italian government might take it away

"**OSTIA IS A** paradise inhabited by demons," reporter Federica Angeli told Index on Censorship.

A half-hour drive from the Colosseum in Rome, this Italian town with a population of 230,000 is where rich footballers set up homes and where Romans have gone on holiday since ancient times. But this relaxed resort is also home to dangerous criminal organisations. People struggle with poverty, they lack access to social housing and three (known) criminal gangs fight over control of the territory. In this environment, journalists are far from safe, as Angeli attests. She is currently under 24-hour police protection.

Angeli was born and raised in Ostia, where she started her career 22 years ago working for a local newspaper. For the past two decades, she has been a crime and legal reporter for La Repubblica, Italy's second-largest newspaper, writing on articles from clandestine dog fights to the illegal arms trade in Rome.

Her troubles started in 2013, when she began an investigation into the criminal organisations operating in Ostia. She did so at a time when the public thought the mafia only came from southern Italy, and the

judiciary was only scratching the surface of Rome's criminal activity.

"Mafia in Rome did not have a name," said Angeli. "If you don't name something, you cannot recognise it, you cannot identify it."

Angeli had been witnessing an increase in criminal activity on her doorstep and decided to find out more about the contracts of beachside lidos, which were being investigated by the judiciary. In May 2013, as she was reporting, Angeli was briefly kidnapped by a member of the Spada family, Armando Spada, who threatened to kill her and her three children, now eight, 10 and 13. She reported the incident to the police and Spada was initially charged with violent threats, but on 15 May a judge pressed more serious charges against him. Spada is now being investigated for violent behaviour, and could face up to four years in jail.

Days before her investigation was due to come out in La Repubblica back in 2013, Angeli woke up in the middle of the night to a woman's screams and the sound of gunfire. When she went to her balcony to investigate, she recognised two members of the Spada clan escaping. She filed a witness report to the police and was told that her witness →

ABOVE: The beautiful beach of Lido di Ostia, in Ostia, near Rome

→ account could be key in bringing charges against the clan. The trial is ongoing and a sentence is expected in November this year. As a result, since 17 July 2013 she has been living with round-the-clock police protection.

Angeli has received many threats over the years. Members of the Spada clan went around her neighbourhood saying she was an *infame*, the word used by the mafia to indicate those who betray them. She was also attacked on social media, being told that she should be thinking about her children.

"These are phrases that are reserved for women," she said. "The fact that a woman was confronting the clan represented a double disgrace."

Once, despite the police protection,

inflammable liquid was thrown into her flat, but she managed to wipe it up and keep her children calm by telling them it was a game.

"I told them they could not get their feet wet and we had to catch the liquid quickly," she said. She found inspiration from the film Life is Beautiful, where the character transforms life in a concentration camp into a game for his son's sake.

She admits she almost gave up, but says she kept going because she felt the support and solidarity of many neighbours. People she had never talked to before started coming out little by little and telling her about how the clans were demanding protection money and threatening local businesses.

"You realise that something is not right

when you see that these people are turning to you for help," said Angeli. "It should be the state who should protect them. What can I guarantee them?"

Her work and her personal sacrifice brought attention to the story of Ostia. There was even a Netflix series released in 2017, Suburra, which shows the underbelly of the resort. In January this year, police in Rome arrested more than 30 members and affiliates of the Spada family on charges of extortion, loan-sharking and drug-trafficking.

Other journalists have been caught in the violence. In November 2017, Roberto Spada head-butted Rai TV reporter Daniele Piervincenzi, breaking his nose, then chased the film crew away with a baton.

Cameraman Edoardo Anselmi was also hit in the head, but continued filming. Piervincenzi was reporting on the alleged relations between politicians and the Spada family ahead of local elections.

In May 2018, another Rai reporter, Nello Trocchia, was attacked while filming the arrests of the Casamonica family, charged with being allied with the Spada clan.

Criminals are not the town's only demons, says Angeli. Some politicians try to discredit the work of reporters and she worries that Italy's current political situation will leave her and other journalists isolated and exposed.

Italy has faced a reshuffle of political forces over the summer after its latest elections, held in March, ended in stalemate. →

RIGHT: Federica Angeli speaking on a panel about journalists under threat at the International Journalism Festival 2018, Perugia

→ With Italy's new prime minister Giuseppe Conte now confirmed, it is worth remembering that the Five Star Movement (M5S), a part of the government, has been vocal in its criticism of the media and has repeatedly named journalists of whose work it does not approve. Beppe Grillo, the comedian who founded the movement in 2009, set up a column known as "Journalist of the Day" on his popular blog. There, Grillo would copy and paste excerpts of articles that he thought portrayed M5S in a negative light. In 2015, Angeli became the victim of an M5S cam-

The threats of these political groups could lead to substantial worsening of our freedom

paign after two local politicians reported her to the anti-mafia commission saying she had backed a left-wing politician who had been later arrested on charges of corruption.

Matteo Salvini, the leader of the far right League, also part of the new government, has railed against journalists. For example, he tweeted that he would remove the "useless police protection" of Roberto Saviano, the author of Gomorrah (an investigation into the

Neapolitan Camorra), who has been under protection since 2006, if they got elected.

"My fear is that the threats of these political groups could lead to substantial worsening of our freedom," Angeli told Index.

Reporters Without Borders ranks Italy at 46 in the World Press Freedom Index, a big advance over the past few years, but it warns that the level of violence against reporters is "alarming and keeps growing". Last December, the ministry of the interior announced that more than 150 journalists received police protection in 2017, while 19 reporters were under round-the-clock police protection. The majority of them work in Rome, a clear sign of the elevated danger of criminal organisations in the Italian capital. In the same month, the ministry of the interior established a "consultation panel" on threats against journalists, with the participation of trade unions and other organisations that represent journalists – the first time a meeting of this kind has happened in Italy.

"In Italy, people have got used to the fact that journalists need police protection," said Angeli.

Though worried about the lack of political support, Angeli has not stopped working. On 6 May, her latest book, A Mano Disarmata (Unarmed), was released. Shortly afterwards, she did a video report for La Repubblica where she showed that villas seized by the state in Ostia from the Casamonica family are still inhabited by members of the clan.

She says it is thanks to the support she receives from her family, fellow journalists and readers that she can keep going.

"Thankfully a powerful 'us' was born," she said. "Without that support, I would not go anywhere. This has helped me get through the hardest moments." ⊗

Irene Caselli is an Italian journalist working between Latin America and Europe and a contributing editor for Index on Censorship magazine

SPECIAL REPORT

Freedom to travel v travel towards freedom

47(02): 39/44 | DOI: 10.1177/0306422018784529

Do travellers care about poor freedom of expression or other rights when they choose where to spend their holidays? Scientist and travel writer **Mark Frary** does the maths

CREDIT: Dr Makkoy/iStock

39
INDEXONCENSORSHIP.ORG

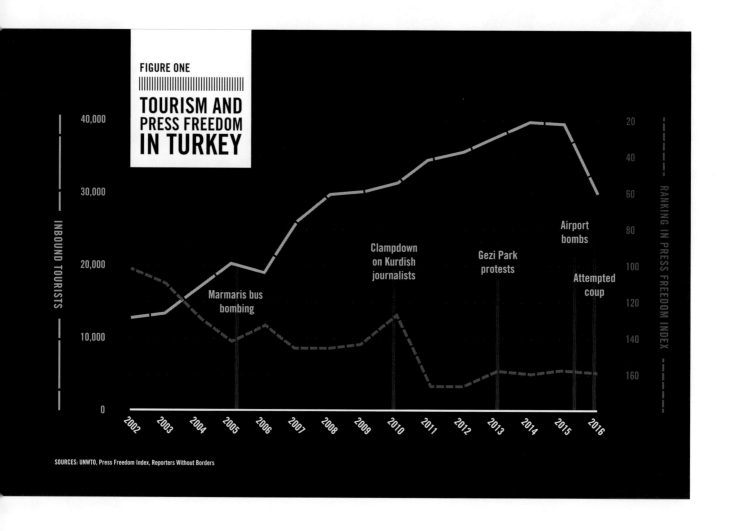

FIGURE ONE

TOURISM AND PRESS FREEDOM IN TURKEY

INBOUND TOURISTS

RANKING IN PRESS FREEDOM INDEX

Marmaris bus bombing

Clampdown on Kurdish journalists

Gezi Park protests

Airport bombs

Attempted coup

SOURCES: UNWTO, Press Freedom Index, Reporters Without Borders

TOURISTS ARE IGNORING a country's slide down the tables evaluating media freedom and other liberties when they book a holiday destination, new analysis shows.

According to data examined for Index, a country might slide down the scale for poor media freedom or freedom of expression, but the number of holidaymakers who visit there appears not to be affected. In fact, some countries see a continuing rise in people heading for their beaches, despite rising violence or increased repression of rights.

But travel expert Justin Francis says this is starting to change as he sees a new generation of travellers who want to find out more about their destination.

While most holidaymakers do not take

issues such as human rights and freedom of expression into account when choosing a destination, there are a growing number who do care, says Francis, founder of tour operating group Responsible Travel. "They think about how their holiday choices might look to others and the wider message they are sending out."

In Mexico, where killings of journalists have risen dramatically in the past six years, tourist numbers continue to rise, hitting 3.5 million visitors in 2016, according to figures from the UN World Tourism Organisation, compared with 2.2 million in 2007.

According to our article on Baja California Sur by Stephen Woodman (see p8), five acts of aggression against

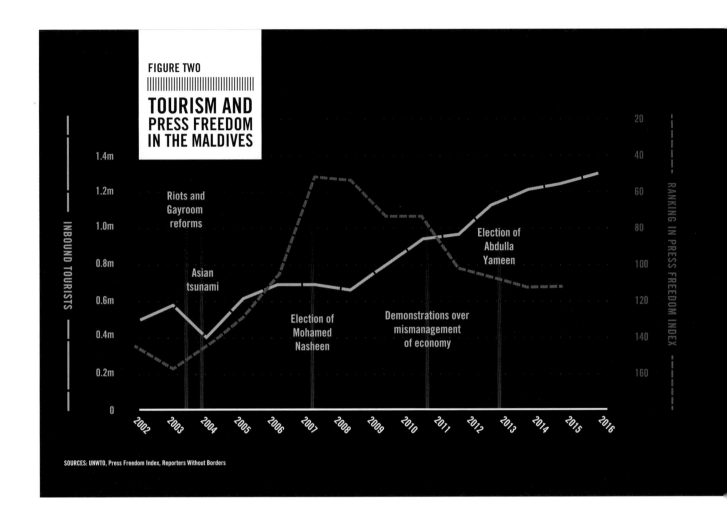

FIGURE TWO

TOURISM AND PRESS FREEDOM IN THE MALDIVES

INBOUND TOURISTS

1.4m
1.2m
1.0m
0.8m
0.6m
0.4m
0.2m
0

Riots and Gayroom reforms

Asian tsunami

Election of Mohamed Nasheen

Demonstrations over mismanagement of economy

Election of Abdulla Yameen

RANKING IN PRESS FREEDOM INDEX

20
40
60
80
100
120
140
160

2002 2003 2004 2005 2006 2007 2008 2009 2010 2011 2012 2013 2014 2015 2016

SOURCES: UNWTO, Press Freedom Index, Reporters Without Borders

journalists were logged by press freedom group Article 19 in the state between 2009 and 2016. This rose to 16 acts of aggression last year, including the murder of Maximino Rodríguez, a crime reporter, who was shot dead in April 2017.

Many media freedom organisations including Index and Reporters Without Borders see Mexico as one of the most dangerous countries in the world for journalists today.

When mapping tourism against freedom of expression and press freedom data, our data analysis regularly shows a dip in traveller numbers when there is a terrorism incident, but no dip when a country's ranking for freedom of expression slides, or when there is a rise in media attacks.

Countries that score best on freedom and feature at the top of the index, led by Switzerland, are all tourism destinations

Mexico is ranked 147th out of 180 in the Reporters Without Borders World Press Freedom Index in 2018, down from 75th in 2002. During this period, tourist numbers have continued to go up.

Meanwhile, in the Maldives – where the government has reduced media freedom, leading to the killing of a journalist and the exile of others – tourist numbers have seen a steady rise since 2009.

→

With this in mind, it is interesting to consider whether we can see any evidence that political events and the loosening, or toughening, of laws governing freedom of expression can affect tourism to leading holiday destinations.

Figures 1 to 3 compare the ranking of countries in the Reporters Without Borders index with inbound tourism statistics from the UN's World Tourism Organisation.

The identification of tourism as a key tool for regimes to generate hard currency to promote their own ideologies means that we can also look more closely at the relationship between tourism and freedom of expression.

We have highlighted a number of key events in the timelines of those countries which reveal that tourists are generally immune to freedom of expression concerns, yet

Argentina reaped huge benefits from being the first country in South America to recognise gay marriage

are highly sensitive to natural disasters and terrorist incidents.

We have taken this further by looking at data collected as part of the annual Human Freedom Index compiled by the Washington-based think-tank, the Cato Institute. The HFI uses 79 distinct indicators of personal and economic freedom, including freedom of expression, identity and relationships and economic freedoms.

This shows that countries that score best on freedom and feature at the top of the index, led by Switzerland, are all tourism destinations. Ian Vasquez, the co-author of the 2018 HFI report, says this is no surprise. So does this mean tourists do favour destinations where there is greater freedom?

"Where does most of the world investment traditionally go? It goes to the countries at the top of the list," said Vasquez. "It doesn't go to where labour is cheapest, it goes to the higher-cost places because they have the most freedom and the best rule of law. People value that, and that shows up in tourism."

While the HFI is aimed at policymakers, academics and journalists, Vasquez believes individuals can also use it to make their decisions.

"Reports like this can make people think twice about where to go. If they do decide to go, even if they are concerned, they will possibly be more thoughtful about their trip."

He cites Cuba as an example. "If more Americans went to Cuba, they would come into contact with ordinary Cubans and it would expand the informal economy, making thousands of Cubans less dependent on the state, and that would be a good thing."

Figure 4, to the right, uses the freedom of expression data collected for the HFI along with World Economic Forum data on how much governments spend on travel and tourism – largely on marketing to overseas tourists through advertising campaigns or by being present at trade shows. The size of the bubbles is relative to the number of inbound tourists.

Egypt, Mexico, Morocco and Thailand all generate a significant proportion of their GDP from tourism and spend heavily to market themselves, even though they score poorly on the HFI.

There are some exceptions to general trends. In 1995, the Burmese government announced that the following year would be Visit Myanmar (Burma) year, with a target of attracting half a million tourists to the country. It is a beautiful country with many natural and man-made attractions.

A travel boycott was called for by Aung San Suu Kyi, leader of Burma's democracy movement at the time, which was supported by organisations globally and was one of the main reasons the government's tourism campaign failed to meet its objectives: just 180,000 tourists visited in 1996.

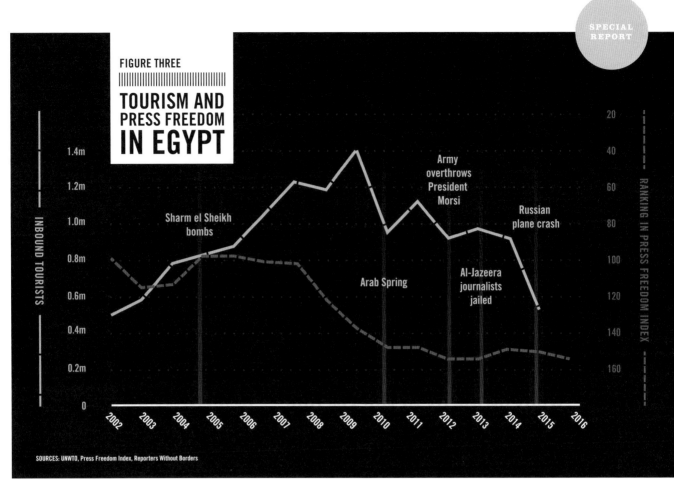

FIGURE THREE

TOURISM AND PRESS FREEDOM IN EGYPT

INBOUND TOURISTS

RANKING IN PRESS FREEDOM INDEX

1.4m
1.2m
1.0m
0.8m
0.6m
0.4m
0.2m
0

20
40
60
80
100
120
140
160

2002 2003 2004 2005 2006 2007 2008 2009 2010 2011 2012 2013 2014 2015 2016

Sharm el Sheikh bombs

Army overthrows President Morsi

Russian plane crash

Arab Spring

Al-Jazeera journalists jailed

SOURCES: UNWTO, Press Freedom Index, Reporters Without Borders

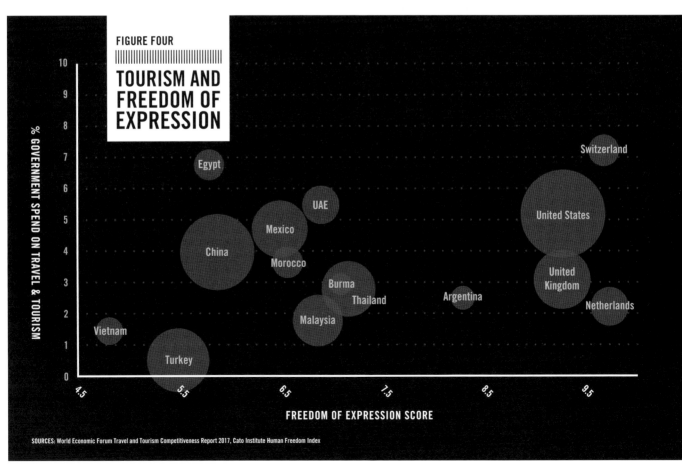

FIGURE FOUR

TOURISM AND FREEDOM OF EXPRESSION

% GOVERNMENT SPEND ON TRAVEL & TOURISM

10
9
8
7
6
5
4
3
2
1
0

Switzerland
Egypt
UAE
Mexico
China
Morocco
Burma
Thailand
Argentina
United States
United Kingdom
Netherlands
Malaysia
Vietnam
Turkey

4.5   5.5   6.5   7.5   8.5   9.5

FREEDOM OF EXPRESSION SCORE

SOURCES: World Economic Forum Travel and Tourism Competitiveness Report 2017, Cato Institute Human Freedom Index

→ who works for the association's judicial department. "Had this kind of performance involved a different religion, such as Islam or Judaism, it [would have] been banned by public powers to avoid a scandal."

Francisco Cases, Bishop of the Diocese of the Canary Islands, reacted via a public letter in which he claimed that the performance had been more upsetting than the crash of a

Tourists come and go and have fun, but freedom of expression is only there for some

Spanair plane from Barcelona to Gran Canaria in 2008, in which 154 people died.

"A blasphemous frivolity has succeeded in […] the gala. It has succeeded in votes, and in the cheers of a heated audience." His words led to a wave of criticism, especially from the Association of Victims of the JK5022 flight. The bishop later said he regretted his words.

The case was filed in December 2017 by a judge at Las Palmas de Gran Canaria's Court of Instruction, Estela María Marrero, who considered that it may have offended some people, but was not against the law.

Nevertheless, the Christian Lawyers Association complained that "more and more people are exceeding the limits of satire by trying to humiliate, to scorn, and even to incite discrimination. They are spreading the idea that anything can be done to Christians, turning us into buffoons". Alejandra Soto claimed "many Christians will not watch or attend the gala after Borja's performance".

In spite of everything, Borja believes "the Canary Islands are indeed a paradise. People are open-minded, tolerant, permissive…". He added: "Carnival means a lot to us, and I don't think our image is being damaged. Quite the contrary, our carnival is like a huge movie set for people around the world to watch our talent." And he does not consider

these legal actions are a threat. "One may feel a bit constricted sometimes, but this feeling is enough to keep doing what you do," he said. "In the end, it is people that have the final say and take their own decisions."

But his has not been the only case of this kind in the Canary Islands recently.

Tenerife activist Roberto Mesa was detained earlier this year for having allegedly committing a crime of insulting the crown. On 7 March, during King Felipe VI's visit to the island, Mesa posted the following comments on his Facebook wall: "Let's feed sharks with the Bourbons" and "Screw Monarchy, the King, and all its repressive bodies."

"A group of policemen broke into my place, broke the door down, handcuffed me and violated my privacy and [that of] my flatmates," Mesa told Index. "They took every electronic device they found. Even notebooks and flags. And now I am afraid. I don't want to spend the rest of my life behind bars."

More than three weeks after being arrested, he had not yet been informed of the

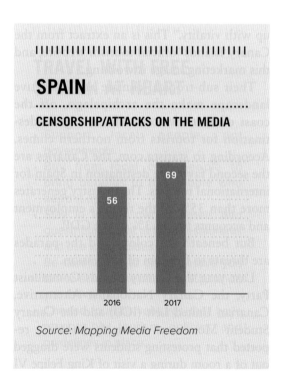

|||||||||||||||||||||||||||||||||||||||||||||

SPAIN

CENSORSHIP/ATTACKS ON THE MEDIA

69

56

2016   2017

Source: Mapping Media Freedom

charges on which he was arrested. "The police did not explain a thing during the arrest," he said. "Once in the police station, I was informed a part of the case is being kept secret and I cannot know what I am accused of. They have been investigating me for six months now and apparently they still don't know enough. I am waiting to be called to testify in Santa Cruz de Tenerife court."

Mesa has faced arrests before. In 2012, he was charged with crimes including public disorder and resistance to the authorities during a plenary session of Santa Cruz de Tenerife's Council. He was also arrested for having allegedly attacked a reporter who was covering a march against oil prospecting works in 2014.

Mesa feels he is in the spotlight. "I don't understand. I am just behaving and thinking as many others," he said.

"This is the third time I have been arrested in the last few years, each new arrest being more disproportionate than the previous one. On the first two occasions, there wasn't even a trial, so it is not unreasonable to think that, for the repressive forces, I am the enemy."

And he is not as positive as Borja regarding the islands' idyllic atmosphere. "Tourists come and go and have fun, but freedom of expression is only there for some," he said. "People who steal, lie, threaten ... do whatever it takes to continue committing atrocities."

Freedom of expression is getting worse throughout Spain, according to many rankings, so the Canary Islands are not a special case. Mesa said: "There is freedom of expression, but only for some. And this is not new, it is only becoming more evident through social media".

And he believes repression will get worse. "The longer we are governed by the right, the more repression we will suffer," he said. "That is why these powers are so afraid of groups of people organising horizontally, without any leaders they can take action against."

But he tries to remain hopeful, saying: "What they don't understand is that arresting one person does not mean people will stop marching and fighting to defend their rights." ✖

Silvia Nortes is a journalist based in Murcia, Spain, and is a regular contributor to Index

CREDIT: Jon Delorme/Picfair

"We're not scared of these things"

47(02): 48/51 I DOI: 10.1177/0306422018784531

Rappler's news editor **Miriam Grace A Go** describes how the Philippine newsroom continues despite all the threats and intimidation, and speaks to Rappler CEO **Maria Ressa** to get her thoughts

MY CHAT CHANNEL with the reporters was particularly frenzied one Tuesday morning back in February. We had played out this scenario before in our conversations — what if, one day, the palace gets so pissed off with us that they stop Pia at the gates? Or boot her out of the press office? — and now it was happening.

Pia Ranada, our reporter covering Philippine President Rodrigo Duterte, was live on Facebook and Twitter documenting how a presidential guard wouldn't let her into Malacañang, the presidential compound, where she had regularly gone since this administration began. There had been an order, but the guard couldn't say from whom.

After 20 minutes, Ranada was allowed into the building where the press office was. She was in for a long day, though. It was the president himself who had ordered the ban, the head of the internal house affairs told Ranada. In fact, she'd been banned from all the buildings in the compound, including the press office. A bit later, it was announced that the ban would cover even our chief executive officer and executive editor, Maria Ressa.

Ranada told me later that she was scared. Her hands were shaking while taking the video. But she was also angry and wanted answers. "I didn't want them to get away with what they were doing," she said.

What happened that day was the culmination of nearly two years of intensified attacks on Rappler, our news website. Those attacks had gone on practically since Duterte had taken office.

Such a twist of fate.

On 9 May 2016, the night of the election, Duterte granted his first interview to Rappler. By October 2016, however, Rappler had gathered solid data to show that his administration was engaging in systematic disinformation, carrying out "social media campaigns meant to shape public opinion, tear down reputations and cripple traditional media institutions", Ressa said as an introduction to a three-part series on the weaponisation of the internet.

A deluge of nasty, personal attacks flooded into her Facebook accounts, inboxes and Twitter. Ressa, the person in the newsroom who most preferred to engage even obvious trolls (a lot of times against our advice), didn't take long to realise that she was talking to people who didn't intend to listen or understand.

"They were just trying to bash me into silence," she said, looking back.

It was ugly. "Maria, you are waste of sperm! Your mother should have swallowed you!"; "Me to the RP Government: Make sure Maria Ressa gets publicly raped to death when Martial law expands to Luzon. It would bring joy in my heart."

The Facebook accounts of some staff, editors and regular contributors were stalked by trolls. Photos of their families were stolen and posted with messages wishing they were murdered and raped. There was one time when a proclaimed Duterte supporter got a photo of our office building on Google Maps and posted it, telling other diehard supporters of the president that this was where they should go in order to harm Rappler employees.

"The whole thing was shocking because we'd never lived through anything like that

Photos of their families were stolen and posted with messages wishing they were murdered and raped

before," Ressa told me. Yet, she asked, which self-respecting journalist wouldn't have written about it? "The data was all there. It was clear. The reason they attacked us was because we were right. In retrospect, it was extremely important for us to have done that story; otherwise, more Filipinos would have been misled." →

OPPOSITE: The perfect sea off the coast of popular tourist island Boracay in the Philippines

→ "What made it difficult was," Ressa realised after the backlash, she was a journalist who "also ran a company."

And, indeed, the government stepped up its attacks and went after the company itself. In Duterte's State of the Nation address in July 2017, he accused Rappler of being foreign-owned. By insisting in subsequent speeches that we were "funded by the CIA" and "fully American-owned", he was laying

What it didn't realise was that, by targeting Rappler, it had roused a bigger enemy

down the argument that we were violating the constitution, which requires media companies to be wholly owned by Filipinos.

By January this year, the Securities and Exchange Commission ordered the company's licence to operate to be revoked (we're still here because we appealed the decision in court). We have also had a cyber libel case filed against us.

"The charges are ludicrous," said Ressa, "but they are complex enough that people can get lost."

Snide remarks designed to make the public doubt Rappler's credibility are loosely made by government officials. During their daily coverage, our reporters have to parry cabinet officials who stop them at press conferences with "Rappler? Haven't you shut down?".

At events attended by the president, organisers must check their lists of journalists coming and strike off any Rappler reporters. In April, one of our reporters, who insisted on covering the National Games in a city more than 400km from Manila, was booted out of a press conference and told by education officials to listen instead to the loudspeakers installed outside.

Lately, state auditors have been releasing reports on individual agencies. Rappler,

like many other news outlets, reported on the findings about questionable contracts, misused funds and unexplained releases. Yet, every time, Duterte's officials would issue a statement singling out Rappler and calling our report "fake news" instead of trying to clear their names of mishandling taxpayers' money. Daily, our journalists receive messages calling them paid hacks who deserve to lose their jobs and get jailed, raped or murdered.

Yet, even in these times, we continue to produce exclusives, getting documents from agencies, inside stories from cabinet officials and briefings from those who remain professional and non-partisan in government. And when reporters worry about losing access to officials, I share with them my principle from when I myself was a reporter: there will always be one other person who knows the information, one other source of those same documents, one other expert who knows an issue like the back of his hand.

The administration may think that it can slow us down with these distractions – yes, the cases are distractions – but what it didn't realise was that, by targeting Rappler, it had roused a bigger enemy. #StandWithRappler has quickly given way to #DefendPressFreedom. Media organisations, here and abroad, have banded together to guard more aggressively against what they see as a creeping attempt to silence dissent here. Campus organisations, even those in schools, and civil-society groups have started organising forums on media literacy and press freedom, requesting to hear from Rappler and other journalists who have experienced the battle with lies and disinformation firsthand.

Something else the administration didn't realise was that when a reporter is freed from physically following Duterte around and sitting through, sometimes, three speeches a day, she has time to work on more substantial stories that scrutinise the government.

When we say it's business as usual at Rappler, we mean it. Sure, we have additional security, both physically and digitally, and

OPPOSITE: Rappler CEO Maria Ressa at a press conference at Rappler's office in Manila, speaking in the wake of the government's decision to revoke their operating licence, January 2018

there are contingency plans in place, but it's the same newsroom where you find people working practically 24/7. Some days, we're crowded at the office when almost everybody has decided to hold meetings at the same time. Some days, someone could bring a skateboard and glide through the newsroom without knocking anybody down because three-quarters of our 100-or-so workforce have decided to work from home.

The reporters jog at night in the park just outside the office. Sometimes I cook for them. Sometimes I remind them to get a day off and recharge.

In between the banter, though, we also ask each other: Why are we holding the line? Why do we keep moving the line? There's a spirit that Rapplers see and reinforce in each other, Ressa points out, that says: "We're not scared of these things."

I had shared with the team how the testing (I don't want to call it a "crisis") of Rappler had made me draw confidence from the fifth verse of the 23rd Psalm: "You prepare a feast for me in the presence of my enemies. You anoint my head with oil." I think it has encouraged some of them, too.

So when, amid the attacks on us,

international recognitions come, one fellow manager would say, "So this is the feast?" I would tell her, "Brace yourself, it's just the appetiser."

And when government agents came to our office to serve notices of investigations and subpoenas, some staff would say, "For clarification, is this still part of Psalm 23?" And they would be told, "This is the 'walking through the valley of the shadow of death'

"The charges are ludicrous," said Ressa, "but they are complex enough that people can get lost"

part." And guess what? We are able to laugh and then focus on our work again.

"The mission of journalism has never been needed as much as it is today," Ressa likes to say. "That's why Rapplers have come back day after day with the best hard-hitting stories they can find. We're stubborn." ⊗

Miriam Grace A Go is an author, award-winning journalist and head of news at Rappler

Slouching away from Eden

47(02): 52/54 I DOI: 10.1177/0306422018784520

Just a few years ago, Turkey was hailed as a role model for the Middle East, with a bright future. But then everything changed. **Kaya Genç** reports on what happened to cool Istanbul

IT SEEMS LIKE only yesterday when Newsweek magazine published a cover story on the city it considered the new hip capital of Europe. A vivid image of two dancers partying hard at a nightclub graced the cover. The headline was assertive but to the point: "Cool Istanbul: Europe's Hippest City Might Not Need Europe After All". It was August 2005. In the Newsweek cover story, trendy clubs Babylon and 360 illustrated Istanbul's entertainment scene; filmmaker Fatih Akın, who won the 2004 Golden Bear at Berlinale the year before, was quoted praising Turkey's rich culture; and the chairwoman of Istanbul's Museum of Modern Art, Oya Eczacibasi, told the magazine how "both Turks and foreigners are excited about the possibilities of the city, which has been a well-kept secret for so long".

The European Union began accession talks with Turkey in December 2004, but the magazine said the country was doing fine without the EU. Turkey was a success story: authentic, entrepreneurial, self-confident.

Coverage of Turkey until 2013 was often this way: an Edenic place waiting to be discovered by foreigners. "Why Turkey is Thriving," said an article in the Project Syndicate; Turkey was a "competitive democracy", according to The New York Times; and The Economist called it a "vibrant democracy with the rule of law". The Financial Times described Turkey as "a dynamic economy led by Islam's equivalent to Christian Democrats".

Such pieces made little mention of Hrant Dink, who was among many intellectuals accused of insulting Turkishness under a new article in the penal code, or the imprisonment of journalist Hakan Albayrak for defaming the memory of Mustafa Kemal Atatürk, or the plight of Mehmet Ali Birand, who faced a criminal investigation for interviewing lawyers of a jailed Kurdish rebel leader.

Alexander Christie-Miller covered Turkey for The Times from 2010 to 2016 and explored the country in The Christian Science Monitor. The experience inevitably altered his view of the country.

"Before I arrived in Turkey, my view was very much shaped by the media and literature I had read in preparation for going there, and also by conversations I had with other journalists who had covered the country," he told Index.

"The impression I formed was that Turkey was a democratising nation coming to terms with its difficult past, and which had immense potential for the future. I had read several recent political histories of the country, such as Hugh and Nicole Pope's Turkey Unveiled, which tended to end on an upbeat note when it came to the dawn of the

AKP [Justice and Development Party] era. I viewed with suspicion those foreigners and Turks who were sceptical of the AKP, and indeed was explicitly warned against [those sceptical of the AKP] by some journalists I spoke to prior to arriving in Turkey."

Then, in 2010, everything changed. A state prosecutor accused a large group of high-ranking military officers of plotting to overthrow the Turkish government, and a

By the end of 2013, positive stories on Turkey had become all but history

darker picture began to emerge. A Turkish newspaper leaked details of a coup plot and published electronic documents listing hundreds of journalists, ordinary Turks and NGO members with claimed links to a shadowy organisation named Ergenekon.

Christie-Miller was among the first to raise the alarm about the authenticity of evidence.

"In my first couple of years, I reported a lot on the Ergenekon and Balyoz cases, which was the main domestic political story at the time. It was clear, especially in the case of Balyoz – which was more straightforward and easier for an outsider to understand than Ergenekon – that there was something seriously amiss about these trials," he said.

The narrative prevalent at the time was that these cases were a kind of "clean hands" reckoning with a dirty past that would aid Turkey's democratisation, but it seemed to Christie-Miller "that the evidence of widespread and highly organised police and judicial corruption seriously complicated this narrative". What surprised him about that whole experience "was the way in which the foreign media as a whole was happy to settle on a single narrative and report that narrative rather than digging into the facts beneath it". →

OPPOSITE: Dancers in Zero nightclub in October 2003 in Istanbul, Turkey, an image featured on the front cover of Newsweek in 2005 (see p54)

ABOVE: Magazine covers from Newsweek from 2005 and The Economist in 2017

2010 marked the start of the slide from paradise, but 2013 became the true annus horribilis for Turkey's representations in the press. The intervening three years had seen solitary voices such as Christie-Miller's interrogate the Turkish judiciary, but with the anti-government protests in the summer of 2013, graver problems with the police force now came to the fore.

Footage of cops burning tents of activists provided the spark that started country-wide protests which left 11 dead and around

2013 became the true annus horribilis for Turkey's representations in the press

8,000 injured. A country that only a few years previously was viewed as a role model in the wake of the Arab Spring was now considered a harbinger of the emergence of majoritarianism in countries including India and the USA. Some later wondered whether the Brexit campaign used tactics similar to those used by Turkish politicians. Both were signs that "liberal democracy, that has long dominated the world [...] is now in the midst of an epic struggle for its own survival",

wrote Yascha Mounk in Slate in a 2016 article entitled The Week Democracy Died.

By the end of 2013, positive stories on Turkey had become all but history. During 2016, Isis and the Kurdistan Workers' Party (PKK) intensified their war on Turkey and, in the eyes of many, Newsweek's "Cool Istanbul: Europe's Hippest City Might Not Need Europe After All" was replaced by "Scary Istanbul: Europe's Most Dangerous City Might Need Europe After All".

Today, Christie-Miller is finishing a book on Turkey. Like many other foreign journalists covering Turkey, he has migrated and spends most of the year in London. He remembers he was covering the Van earthquake in 2011, and the government's response to it, when he decided "Turkish politics was a zero-sum game in which the various actors were unable to look beyond their own narrow interests, even following a tragedy that entailed substantial loss of life".

Looking back at this, he added: "I am struck now by my own naivety, more than anything else."

The change in Turkey's representations was swift and awkward and it recently became the subject of academic research. İlker Birbil, a professor of industrial engineering at Sabancı University, analysed 1,472 articles and 44 editorials in The New York Times about Turkey's rulers between 1 January 2004 and 10 October 2014. Birbil found that the most positive editorial was posted during the 2011 elections that resulted in the governing party's victory; the lowest point, meanwhile, was April 2014, when the Turkish government closed down access to Twitter.

It is difficult to guess whether Turkey can once again be the Edenic, hip, cool place it was in 2005, but for those who live in Turkey one thing is clear: here the past has indeed become a foreign country. ⊗

Kaya Genç is the contributing editor (Turkey) for Index on Censorship magazine

White sands, dark deeds

47(02): 55/57 I DOI: 10.1177/0306422018784534

The reputation of the Maldives as a fantasy holiday idyll is only half the picture. Ahead of September's elections, **Zaheena Rasheed** reports on the persecution that lies behind those pictures of perfect beaches

IF YOU WERE to search Twitter for what people were saying about the Maldives on any given day, you would get two types of posts. On the one hand are pictures of the world's wealthy sipping cocktails on palm-fringed beaches, snorkelling in shimmering turquoise waters or lounging in underwater spas as colourful fish swim overhead. On the other are images of riot police gassing and beating protesters, and pleas from Maldivians for freedom for jailed dissidents, as well as demands for justice for attacks on bloggers and journalists.

These search results are a perfect example of the dual realities that mark the present-day Maldives.

To holidaymakers, the Maldives is paradise – a place where one goes to retreat from the world. Indeed, upmarket hotels advertise the Indian Ocean archipelago as a "deserted idyll" and "unspoiled wilderness", where guests can take off their shoes, switch off the news, "embrace tranquillity" and "treat yourself to paradise".

Those descriptions could not be further from the truth for ordinary Maldivians.

President Abdulla Yameen, who assumed power following a disputed election in 2013, has rolled back the country's hard-won democratic gains; jailed, or forced into exile, nearly all opposition leaders; banned protests; shuttered newspapers; and, according to critics, allowed radical Islam to flourish.

Meanwhile, journalists based in the country say they are finding it increasingly difficult to report there. The "disappearance" of a journalist, the killing of a blogger, death threats, imprisonment and hefty fines are placing an enormous pressure on those who seek to inform the public about what is going on. The threats to safety, coupled with the government's refusal to answer questions, has made reporting on topics such as corruption, rights abuses and growing Islamic extremism near-impossible.

Yet it is likely that the president may stand virtually unopposed as Maldivians head to the ballot box to elect a president in September this year.

How did we get here?

It began when the country's first democratically elected president, Mohamed Nasheed, was ousted in 2012. Three years later, he was jailed on terrorism charges. The trial triggered mass protests, resulting in the arrest of hundreds of people, the prosecution of more opposition figures and a near-total ban on demonstrations and political →

ABOVE: Riot policemen block an area during a protest by supporters of former President Mohamed Nasheed near parliament in Male, Maldives

→ rallies. Journalists, activists and lawyers reported receiving death threats and a journalist disappeared, but none of the cases was successfully investigated or prosecuted.

The next year, in 2016, a massive corruption scandal engulfed Yameen following revelations that his deputy coordinated the theft of more than US$79m in revenues from island sales.

Yameen denies the corruption allegations. Pleading ignorance, he blamed the embezzlement of state coffers on his vice-president, who he sacked and jailed on graft (political corruption for personal gain) and terrorism charges. As accusations of politicised trials piled up, judges moved to silence criticism by suspending lawyers en masse on contempt of court charges and barring journalists from the courts.

Meanwhile, parliament, where the ruling party holds a majority, passed a law criminalising speech that was defamatory or deemed a threat to national security and religious unity.

His popularity plunging, Yameen has styled himself as the sole defender of Islam in the Sunni-majority country, and labelled any foreign criticism as interference aimed at undermining Islam. He has pledged to end a six-decade moratorium on the death penalty and to crack down on what he calls anti-Islamic speech.

When Yameen Rasheed, a young blogger who criticised authoritarianism and growing religious violence, was stabbed to death in April last year, the president condemned those who "insult Islam", saying there were limits to free speech. The next month, the police placed three other bloggers, all of whom live abroad, under investigation on unspecified charges.

Taken together, critics say Yameen's actions have resulted in a climate of fear that does not bode well for the prospect of free and fair elections.

Journalists, activists and dissidents say they face hefty fines, jail, assault and even death for criticising the president and his allies.

Hussain Fiyaz Moosa, the chief executive officer of Raajje TV, says the main tool used by the government to quash criticism is the Anti-Defamation Law passed in 2016. Since the law came into effect, the broadcast regulator has fined the opposition-aligned station MVR1.7m ($109,718), mainly for defaming the president.

In one instance, the station was punished when it aired a speech in which an opposition politician accused Yameen of failing to deliver on his development pledges.

"Over the space of three years, how many billions of rufiyaa have been handed to him from the state coffers? But nothing has been done. We have seen nothing but theft and corruption," the remarks that caused offence read, according to Raajje TV.

Ironically, the politician responsible for the offensive remarks was not penalised. But Raajje TV was warned that it could face closure if it failed to pay the fine, forcing the station's staff to canvass on the streets to raise the money needed.

"Because of these massive fines, we cannot invite certain guests on air or cover certain topics, including corruption, theft [or] misuse of state resources by senior officials of the state, especially President Yameen and his wife. Even when we have evidence," said Fiyaz. This is not the station's only worry. Raajje TV's journalists are regularly subject to government harassment, including arrest and prosecution.

Meanwhile, suspects in a near-fatal attack on station anchor Ibrahim Asward Waheed, in 2012, and an arson attack that destroyed the station's headquarters the following year are yet to be prosecuted.

"All of this has put us on the back foot," said Fiyaz. "The government is using all means possible to shut us down ... We have no protection."

The government has also moved to silence criticism on social media. In March 2017, Shammoon Jaleel, an opposition supporter, fled the Maldives fearing persecution for criticising a planned government deal to lease a central atoll to Saudi Crown Prince Mohammed bin Salman, one of Yameen's backers on the international stage. Jaleel,

who has a following of more than 20,000 on Twitter, had already spent more than 40 days in jail the previous year for likening riot police to animals.

Jaleel says he left the Maldives after receiving death threats via Twitter and text messages.

"I was also getting calls and I was told I would be killed inside my own house. I was getting harassed on the streets by members of gangs. And then I was summoned to the police and my phone was confiscated on charges of inciting hate. That's when I left," the 29-year-old said.

Another activist, Thayyib Shaheem, who angered the government with leaks of sensitive plans, said that his phone number was

He has pledged to end a six-decade moratorium on the death penalty and to crack down on what he calls anti-Islamic speech

disconnected and reassigned to a third party, who had changed the passwords of his social media account using the number. Later, it emerged that police had accessed the activist's phone's sim card through a court order. Shaheem now lives in exile in Sri Lanka.

"The government is pushing the image that the Maldives is a peaceful tourist destination, that it's a young democracy undergoing a transition. But the ground reality could not be more different," said Mariyam Shiuna, executive director at anti-corruption group Transparency Maldives.

"The future looks bleak. With serious doubts over the upcoming election, we are either heading to a long period of instability or a long period of authoritarianism." ⊗

Zaheena Rasheed is the former editor of the Maldives Independent and an Index on Censorship journalism award winner in 2017

IN FOCUS

IN THIS SECTION

MAIN: An Iraqi journalist on the scene after an Isis suicide bomber attacked an
Iraqi special forces unit during clashes in Bartella, east of Mosul, 2016

After Isis lost

47(02): 60/62 | DOI: 10.1177/0306422018784509

An Iraqi journalist tells **Laura Silvia Battaglia** how reporting in Iraq is tougher now than it was in the 1970s

WITH DECADES OF experience as journalists in Iraq under their belts, Ali al-Jafal and his son, Oteil, have seen many things change in their country. But one thing remains a constant: the extreme difficulty of working in one of the most dangerous countries in the world for journalists. It continues to be very easy to get yourself killed for not self-censoring and for daring to report in a negative way on prominent political figures.

The pair, from Baghdad, have been working for many years in both local and international media. Ali, now 60, has been a journalist since 1979 and is mainly a writer on cultural, political and society-related themes. He believes the current situation is "considerably more complicated and dangerous now than it was [in the 1970s], even though in those days we were under a dictatorship".

"In my time, there was a ministry of information. This meant that there was censorship but it was perfectly centralised, as in a closed circuit," he said. "It was possible to talk, for example, about internal problems, or the scarcity of services for citizens, but without ever mentioning as a cause, or pointing the finger at members of, the Ba'ath Party and, even more so, at the president, Saddam Hussein.

"Nowadays, the censorship business has multiplied. Since the ministries are assigned to different parties and … corruption is a common denominator, responsibility for any type of complaint falls on the journalist – putting him in danger of his life or of losing his job."

We meet in Baghdad near where they both live. The city has changed massively in recent years and is no longer the war-ravaged city some people might expect. Instead, old districts such as Mutanabbi Street on the Tigris River – full of bookshops and coffee houses – compete with new commercial areas such as Mansour and Jadriya, with huge shopping centres, cinemas, restaurants and hotels. The al-Jafal family lives in Talbiyah, a neighbourhood of old houses and dirt roads similar to the majority of the suburbs in Baghdad.

Oteil, 31, who has been in journalism since 2004 and currently works at Al Iraqiya TV as an editor in the political section, agrees with his father's view that things are getting worse. Both men say the past year has been particularly bad. Due to the military conflict with Isis, journalists have found themselves caught between politics and the business interests of the media industry, and have often paid bitterly.

"After the advent of the Islamic State, many satellite channels obliged us to cover the war. [This was] without our having ever received, nor the companies having organised, adequate training for us," said Oteil.

"Many did not encourage or oblige us to

Many did not encourage or oblige us to wear essential protection such as helmets and bulletproof vests

wear essential protection such as helmets and bulletproof vests and, obviously, did not budget for them."

This situation has resulted in the deaths of dozens of colleagues, photographers and cameramen. "Many of us refused, for example, to go to the frontline," he said. "And if we refused, the company managers threatened us with dismissal. I myself was subjected to this threat." So Oteil went to the frontline.

This was commonplace. In October 2014, I trained 50 journalists all over the country for work on the battlefield, distributing a survey as part of this training. All those journalists belonged to the main media from Baghdad, Samarra and Karbala. Most of them were young and male and told me that they were pushed, and at times forced, to go to the battlefield. →

OPPOSITE: A local, young award-winning photographer Qamar Hashim takes pictures in Baghdad, 2011

CREDIT: Thaier al-Sudani/Reuters

→ At that time, all of them went without body armour or helmets. They didn't know how much time the assignment would take. Not one of them had any training before this, and no one knew basic first aid. One of my students saw his colleague dying in battle and couldn't save his life. He didn't want to go back to the frontline and, for that reason, his career took a step back.

Oteil was fortunate to survive. Others were not, and a name has emerged, "information martyr", for those journalists who have lost their lives on the battlefield.

"The families of the information martyrs have been treated as less than nothing," said Oteil. "They do not receive any supplementary monthly salary, nor any aid from the

It is almost impossible to avoid propaganda. If you fight against it, you will experience threats and kidnapping

state, nor from the media in which these fathers of families were employed… the politicians and companies in turn use them to cite them when they need to, when self-glorifying their own contribution to this military campaign."

Iraq currently ranks 160th out of 180 countries on the Reporters Without Borders 2018 World Press Freedom Index, down two places from 2017. Journalists are often targeted by gunmen from pro-government militias, as well as militant groups including Isis. The murder of journalists usually goes unpunished, with investigations, if they occur, resulting in little justice.

Of militias, Oteil said: "Every party has its own. If you make a mistake, they stake out your house, they threaten you, they abduct you. One way or another, they make you pay dearly for it."

So, in order to work in today's Iraq, is self-censorship becoming essential?

Oteil believes that "in Iraq, currently, one cannot write freely, but rather has to follow the political agenda imposed on the channels' employees, on pain of dismissal".

It is almost impossible to avoid propaganda. If you fight against it, you will experience threats and kidnapping. That's the reason why investigative journalism is very difficult to practise in this country.

Even just getting around poses a risk for journalists, as security permits are difficult to obtain and are essential for reporters going about their business.

"Iraqi streets are full of army and police vehicles and checkpoints: many of our colleagues have been arrested for lack of a card, a stamp, a permit, simply because it is difficult to obtain them," said Oteil. "Just as it is difficult to obtain access to transparent information from state institutions or to statistics."

In June the Iraqi authorities issued a warrant for the arrest of journalist Hossam al-Kaabi for stealing documents. The journalist went into hiding, saying the documents were public and he had been quoting them in an investigation. And all this is happening because "despite the country being formally a democracy, an oligarchic logic prevails and there is a subdivision of power among the parties", said Oteil. Each of these parties and interest groups tries to use its power for its own propaganda, employing national media channels, alongside its own private channels, social media and advertisements to advance its own cause.

He even questions the role of the journalists' union now. "It is considerably more concerned with being a showcase for the powerful than a structure capable of defending our rights." ⊗

Laura Silvia Battaglia is an award-winning freelance journalist based between Iraq, Yemen and Italy. She is a contributing editor to Index

Sunshine capital

47(02): 63/65 I DOI: 10.1177/0306422018784510

As the UK approves new measures to tackle money laundering in the British Virgin Islands, **Davion Smith** discusses other secrecy issues that make it difficult for reporters to discover the truth

WITH A COMMANDING majority of the population in the British Virgin Islands being expatriates, hardly any of the mainstream local media journalists are BVI natives. Coming predominantly from countries with established freedom of information laws, they are inducted into a society where accessing information is challenging. This is because such information laws do not currently exist in this UK Overseas Territory, despite calls for their implementation.

Few know the difficulties associated with the absence of these laws better than broadcast journalist Zan Lewis, who has been reporting there for more than 18 years.

"Getting information has always been difficult, particularly when you're getting information from government. Government is known to sift certain information," he said.

Cultural protocol for getting information on matters of governance and public record usually requires journalists to contact the government departments responsible for that subject. The reporter then talks to officers who are often wary of providing any information.

This unrelenting reluctance stems from a fear of government retaliation, which could mean losing their jobs. So, to fend off enquiring reporters, public servants occasionally use the phrase: "We've been instructed not to speak with the media."

"There might be information that, probably, would be public information that nobody is trying to hide," said Freeman Rodgers, editor of the BVI Beacon newspaper. "But, in the absence of a clear-cut system and a law saying 'this is public' and 'this is not public', then I think public officers tend to err on the side of caution and would usually prefer not to give you whatever information you might be after."

Of course not all information is necessarily harmless, and without freedom of information it's hard to know where corruption lies.

This country has already witnessed a scandal – albeit one away from government control – in which difficulty in accessing information was pivotal. These small Caribbean islands, with a population of roughly 30,000, were at the centre of the Panama Papers offshore tax haven revelations back in 2016. Last month, it was announced that British overseas territories, including the BVI, would be forced to reveal ownership of companies based there after the UK approved new measures to tackle money-laundering and corruption. The move will force them to make public the owners of all companies registered there by the end of 2020.

There have also been personal instances where contacting government departments for records resulted in passing the proverbial buck. On one occasion I was directed to the minister responsible for the subject. The minister was keen to redirect me to →

ABOVE: Yachts in a bay in the island of Virgin Gorda, British Virgin Islands

→   the permanent secretary in the ministry, who then directed me to a sub-departmental head. Before long, and without making much headway, I was rerouted back to the original minister.

With this way of life, investigating operations of government here in the British Virgin Islands has sometimes resulted in superficial reporting. Practising in what can be described as an unfriendly media environment BVI journalists rely on information from whistleblowers who often insist on speaking anonymously. This has caught the attention of the Premier of the Virgin Islands, Daniel Orlando Smith, who noted increased occurrences of whistleblowing and has claimed the territory does have "freedom of information".

"Even if I don't put a document out there it gets out there, so that is freedom of information," he argued, while speaking at a media conference earlier this year.

Despite the absence of these fundamental laws, and despite the associated challenges,

Freeman and Lewis have both reported that the ease of accessing information on these islands has improved over the years. They attributed this improvement to the increase in calls for freedom of information legislation.

"When I first got here 12 years ago, we always made this call for it. For a while, it seemed like we were just asking for it and nobody was really listening, but now I think people are starting to listen and people are starting to understand the importance of it and I think that has helped make information more accessible," said Freeman, who migrated from the USA to practise in the BVI.

Over the years, calls for the legislation have come from former complaints commissioner the late Elton Georges and former governor John Duncan, among others.

Recently appointed BVI Governor Augustus Jaspert has taken on the mantle to have the law implemented. While delivering his Speech from the Throne, a tradition where the government sets out its upcoming

implementing these laws, the current government faces numerous criticisms about lack of transparency and accountability.

These criticisms are not without merit, given that the press – and, by extension, the public – has been unable to exhaustively scrutinise the operations of the BVI government for roughly a decade. Up to 2017, the government had not produced financial audits or reports for some 10 years and is now in the process of drafting retroactive reports.

Criticisms have even come from within the Smith administration and have subsequently caused a rift between members in government. According to a March 2018 BVI News

This unrelenting reluctance to provide information stems from a fear of government retaliation, which could mean losing their jobs

agenda, in the BVI parliament in March, Jaspert pledged to have a Freedom of Information Bill introduced in the territory's House of Assembly before the end of this year.

"This piece of legislation will allow for increased transparency and accountability of public affairs," he said. "The bill includes recommendations for the establishment of a Freedom of Information Unit to provide the public with the appropriate administrative mechanism to make and receive requests."

However, this is not the first time such a bill has been promised. According to the BVI Beacon archives, promises to implement this law date as far back as 2004.

The paper reported that, in 2004, a Law Reform Commission had submitted a report to the BVI government recommending freedom of information legislation.

Since that time, two administrations have been in power, but neither appears to have made any headway in implementing the law. And while the BVI still lags behind in

online report, members within the government claimed the BVI premier had initiated certain activities in government ministries and departments "without the knowledge and consent of ministers who constitutionally hold responsibility for those subjects".

The government has also faced criticism from the parliamentary opposition. Other Caribbean nations such as St Kitts and Nevis, Jamaica, Guyana, Trinidad and Tobago and the Dominican Republic have already implemented freedom of information laws.

With what can be described as glaring examples of questionable governance in the BVI, the calls for freedom of information legislation continue to grow. This increase is welcomed among the small fraternity of journalists who argue that freedom of information promotes accountability, transparency and good governance. ⊗

Davion Smith is a reporter at BVI News, *based on the island of Tortola*

Demonising those teenage dirtbags

47(02): 66/69 | DOI: 10.1177/0306422018784511

From jazz to rap, the establishment always wants to ban new styles of music with little reason, writes **Jon Savage**

THEY'RE AT IT again: worrying that music is indoctrinating young people and sending them down a slippery slope to hell. In April, Amber Rudd, then British home secretary, issued a statement about an upsurge in violent youth crime, linking it to the influence of drill music – a form of contemporary urban rap – and calling on the music industry to be "a positive influence".

With its violent lyrics and gang themes, drill might appear dangerous to alarmed adults. Like much rap over the last 35 years, it sees the world as a dog-eats-dog struggle that all too accurately describes life for the poor under neo-liberalism. It aims to be frightening and has succeeded all too well.

But this flap about a new musical style is nothing new. Like rock'n'roll, and jazz before that, moralists and politicians have always pointed to music as having a terrifying influence on young people.

Before World War I, a powerful reform movement in the USA targeted the "animal dances" – fads inspired by animal movements, including the turkey trot – that exploded in popularity with the success of ragtime. As one campaigner fulminated: "It has struck sex o'clock in America; a wave of sex hysteria and sex discussion seems to have invaded this country."

In the early 1920s, the Ladies' Home Journal launched an anti-jazz crusade which castigated "the sensuous stimulation of the abominable big jazz orchestra with its voodoo-born minors and its direct appeal to the sensory centre".

The actual legislation against jazz music in the 1920s was minor and localised (reformists were preoccupied with Prohibition), but it didn't stop the moralists. In the late 1930s, the popularity of swing culture was excoriated by the Catholic bishop of Dubuque, Iowa, who denounced swing as "evil" and "communistic".

"We permit jam sessions, jitterbugs and cannibalistic rhythm orgies to occupy a place in our social scheme of things, wooing

our youth along the primrose path to hell," he said.

These concerns were used by Harry J Anslinger – the first commissioner of the US Treasury Department's Federal Bureau of Narcotics – to mount a campaign against jazz-associated drugs, in particular marijuana.

Each new generational music style attracts adverse attention. Unmanliness and excessive sexuality were constant charges that began

The hypnotic rhythm and the wild gestures have a maddening effect on a rhythm-loving age group

in the mid 1920s with the early pop icon and sex symbol, Rudolph Valentino. Frank Sinatra was vilified for being ineligible for military service during World War II; Elvis Presley was hit by a storm of hostility in the USA during 1956 for his directness and apparent sensuality. That same year, rock'n'roll was banned in the Californian town of Santa Cruz, where, after a concert by Chuck Higgins and his Orchestra, city authorities called it "detrimental to both the health and morals of our youth and community".

When Bill Haley's Rock Around the Clock showed in British cinemas during the late summer of that year, outbreaks of petty hooliganism resulted in sensational headlines. As one reader wrote to The Times at the time: "The hypnotic rhythm and the wild gestures have a maddening effect on a rhythm-loving age group and the result of its impact is the relaxing of all self control." The film was promptly banned in cities around the country.

The 1960s saw the volume and incidence of these moral panics increase, just as youth began to find their power as a market force and class. In 1964, the Mods and Rockers disturbances at British seaside resorts gave rise to a textbook case of moral panic about violence and drugs. Two-and-a-half years →

OPPOSITE: Elvis Presley, who was accused of being too sensual, with female fans, Florida, 1956

→ after the Mod panic, the onset of the drug culture in popular music during late 1966 and early 1967 gave moralisers and newspapers a fresh target.

The topic of psychedelic drugs blew open

Teenagers are hardwired, at various times, to play society's dominant values back at adults and the authorities in a raw manner

ABOVE: Teenagers burn Beatles' records, books and wigs in response to John Lennon's comment that The Beatles were more popular than Jesus, Georgia, USA

after the arrest of the Rolling Stones on drug charges in February 1967. Several singles were banned or subject to hostile scrutiny early that year: records by The Rolling Stones, as well as by EMI groups The Game, The Smoke and Pink Floyd had been censored or critically lashed for their portrayal of sex, drugs and transvestitism respectively.

Even The Beatles fell foul of this censorious climate, when the song A Day In The Life was banned by the BBC during May. One month later, Paul McCartney went on national television and admitted that he had taken LSD.

The effect of hostile media reportage was to alert the police and the authorities and to make them see this new youth manifestation as a threat. The same thing occurred in the late 1980s when a tabloid panic about ecstasy and acid house music fed into the authorities' concerns about illegal raves. After the week-long Castlemorton Common Festival in May 1992, the Conservatives introduced the Criminal Justice and Public Order Act (1994), which explicitly targeted the "repetitive beats" of house music.

With a century-long history of moral panics and bans – both of which have had little effect except to focus the young even more on their chosen music – it's clear that censorship of music is a temporary, and unsatisfactory, solution that attacks the surface manifestation rather than a deeper problem.

Teenagers are hardwired, at various times, to play society's dominant values back at adults and the authorities in a raw manner. Thus punk's shocking arrival – swearing, ragged clothes and an aggressive demeanour – coincided with the 1970s wave of youth unemployment. As Johnny Rotten sang on the Sex Pistols' God Save The Queen: "We are the flowers in your dustbin."

Instead of condemning young people for reflecting the world through their lyrics, adults and authorities need to listen to their concerns. Their music may be rebarbative, and even unpalatable, but they're telling you something you need to know. ⊗

Jon Savage is a music journalist, author and broadcaster, who wrote the award-winning book England's Dreaming: The Sex Pistols and Punk Music, as well as Teenage: The Creation of Youth 1875-1945 and 1966: The Year the Decade Exploded

PICTURED: Rapper Cardi B, known for her sexual-ised lyrics, performs at the iHeart Radio Jingle Ball, December 2017

Under the watchful eye of the army

47(02): 70/72 | DOI: 10.1177/0306422018784512

Ahead of July's elections, **Samira Shackle** assesses how Pakistan's military has the media in its sights

TAHA SIDDIQUI WAS on a busy road in the Pakistani city of Rawalpindi in January when two vehicles blocked his car on both sides. Surrounded by armed men, he realised it was a kidnap attempt and made a dash for it, running through incoming traffic, trying to dive into a cab and crawling through undergrowth.

Siddiqui, a journalist critical of Pakistan's military establishment, had no doubt about who was after him. For at least five years, he had been receiving calls from military personnel warning him about his stories and online posts. In 2017, a legal case had been registered against him for maligning the military on social media.

As soon as he reached safety, Siddiqui tweeted photos of himself, dishevelled and bloodstained, and called a press conference to denounce the crackdown on freedom of speech.

"I wanted to go public, to tell not just fellow Pakistanis but the world what they do with journalists in Pakistan," he told Index.

The stakes were high: an abduction by the intelligence apparatus often ends with a body dumped at the side of the road.

"I felt that it could provide me some security, given that they had not finished the job," said Siddiqui. "I wanted to ensure that they knew the whole world was watching."

The brazen assault on Siddiqui was part of a serious clampdown on free expression in Pakistan, especially targeted at the media, which analysts have tied to July's general election. The military establishment has long been Pakistan's centre of power, and it is keen to shore up its authority.

"Pakistan is known to have a poor record on democracy," said Siddiqui. "In the coming months, the military wants to come back into the driving seat – and for that it needs to tame the media, the politicians, the activists."

Over the past year, numerous journalists and social media activists – mostly liberal, secular and critical of the military – have been abducted by agents of the state, tortured and held for several weeks. If they are released, they tend to give up blogging and stop criticising the military or the hardline religious groups that the military uses as proxies in its various geopolitical struggles.

In January 2017, security forces abducted five men – Salman Haider, Waqas Goraya, Aasim Saeed, Ahmed Raza Naseer and Samar Abbas – who were critics of militant religious groups and Pakistan's security establishment. Four were released after three weeks of public protests. Samar Abbas remains forcibly disappeared.

As the election approaches, certain topics are completely off-limits. The elected prime minister, Nawaz Sharif – a vocal critic of the

military – was ousted in July 2017 over a corruption scandal. In a remarkable example of direct censorship, Pakistan's TV channels intermittently turned off the sound during coverage of a speech he gave on 16 April 2018. In the same month, the country's most popular TV news channel, Geo, was taken off air, reportedly over its favourable coverage of Sharif. It was returned only after a deal in which Geo agreed to tone down its reporting.

"What was implicit before is now explicit," said one Geo journalist who asked to remain anonymous. "It's quite clear. If we want to remain on air and protect our personal safety, we have to toe the line."

Meanwhile, a growing protest movement by the country's ethnic Pashtun population, which explicitly criticises the army over its "war-on-terror" tactics targeted at Pashtuns, has been subject to a mainstream-media blackout. Columnists at major newspapers – including The News, Pakistan's biggest English-language daily and part of the same media group as Geo – have complained of

I wanted to go public, to tell not just fellow Pakistanis but the world what they do with journalists in Pakistan

having their columns censored or held back.

"This kind of environment means that mainstream media credibility is truly at stake," said Raza Rumi, a Pakistani journalist who lives in the USA following an attempted assassination in 2014.

"They don't have express written formal orders by anyone, but they're indulging in self-censorship, which goes against the tenets of public journalism."

Rumi, who remotely edits the Pakistan-based Daily Times, acknowledges that he has self-censored, too.

"I am safe, I'm out of the country, →

OPPOSITE: Protesters in Lahore in April 2018 call out the government on forced disappearances by intelligence agencies

→ but I worry about my colleagues on the ground. So you hold things, or you prune and soften the language."

Pakistan has a long history of a controlled media, but this crackdown comes after several decades of rapid liberalisation. Pakistan's modern media industry was born in 2002, after President General Pervez Musharraf allowed the licensing of private broadcasters.

Until then, there was only one news channel, the state-run PTV. Now, there are scores.

Imran Aslam, president of Geo News, told me in 2015 that when he was a newspaper editor in the 1980s, state censorship entailed army men literally standing behind journalists as they readied pages for print. He protested by printing blank pages or by burying

The military wants to come back to the driving seat – and for that it needs to tame the media

censored stories in the classified ads. In the intervening decades, the media became more free and critical than ever before, although certain topics, such as religion, sexuality and the intelligence services always remained off-limits.

Nonetheless, this increased freedom caused a major shift in the nature of public life that coincided with Pakistan's return to democracy in 2008. The country's leaders had to answer for policies, mistakes and crimes in a way they never had to before.

"Pakistan entered a new democratic moment, but it was always one step forward, two steps back," said Rumi. "And now we are seeing a return to full-throttle censorship."

Pakistan is ranked 139 out of 180 countries on the World Press Freedom Index 2018. There are numerous restrictions on freedom of expression: the threat of reprisal from terrorist organisations or the militant

wings of political parties, and the "deep state". Understanding the power and reach of this "deep state" requires some knowledge of Pakistan's history – this is a country that has spent more than 30 of its 70 years under military dictatorship. Even when civilian politicians are ostensibly in control, as they are now, the military is running things behind the scenes.

"The Pakistani media fears the military so much that it has started self-censoring more than it should," said Siddiqui. "So now, even issues that would be covered before and would not irritate the army are being ignored."

There have been some attempts at pushback. The protests by the Pashtun Tahafuz Movement came about through a grassroots campaign by young people, mostly in their 20s. The leaders of the movement have circumvented media blackouts by using Twitter and Facebook Live videos to broadcast their rallies and other activities.

Meanwhile, more than 100 journalists have signed a petition protesting against media houses' capitulation to the authorities through censoring and removing content.

"People within the media and these protest movements are challenging this increasing authoritarianism. But without the civilian government or judiciary taking action, it is hard to see things seriously improving," said Rumi.

Like Rumi, Siddiqui is now in exile, living in France where he is launching a media watchdog to track self-censorship in south Asian newsrooms. He cannot visualise a return to Pakistan.

"I want to be alive, and they might shoot me at the airport if I go back, given that now I have become even more vocal about military abuses," he said. "I want to continue talking about my country, and my region, and I believe the only way I can continue doing so is from the safety of exile." ⊗

Samira Shackle is a freelance journalist and deputy editor of New Humanist

Liberté, egalité... autorité

47(02): 73/77 I DOI: 10.1177/0306422018784513

One of the forefathers of democratic principles, the French government, is abandoning that heritage, writes **Jean-Paul Marthoz**

"**FRANCE,**" **AS FORMER** socialist justice minister Robert Badinter acidly put it, "is not the fatherland of human rights. It is the fatherland of the declaration of human rights."

But right now, France's democractic leadership is under scrutiny, with journalists being stopped from reporting and new laws giving wide-ranging extra powers to the police. This is all the more worrying since President Emmanuel Macron was elected on a promise to be a liberal, committed to confront the authoritarian trends represented by both the National Front and the radical left, and a pro-European, determined to roll back the populist movements from Hungary to Italy.

Macron, a candidate who upset the traditional and exhausted mainstream parties and stood up to the far right, was expected to have done more by now to set out a new democratic vision.

During the 2017 presidential campaign, Macron promised to be the hero of press freedom. He was described by many →

ABOVE: Emmanuel Macron, head of the political movement En Marche !, while he was a candidate for the 2017 French presidential election

ABOVE: The other Statue of Liberty, on the Seine in Paris

CREDIT: Matthieu Photoglovsky/iStock

→ journalists as a liberal candidate who would inject some fresh air in a country where the "*raison d'état*" is not a joke.

Since Charles De Gaulle and the inauguration of the Fifth Republic, the French presidency acts as a form of elective monarchy.

President Nicolas Sarkozy (2007-2012) tried to bring the media to heel, and under his remit the directors of public broadcasting were directly chosen by the Elysée and a number of investigative journalists were allegedly put under surveillance by the secret service.

His Socialist successor, President François Hollande (2012-2017) liked schmoozing with the press. He even confided in two Le Monde journalists who published a bestseller whose title said it all: "*Un président ne devrait pas dire ça.*" (A president should not say that).

Macron appeared to announce a presidency which would not only distance itself from these flawed models of press/power relationships, but also from the media-bashing crowd: Jean-Luc Mélenchon, of the left-wing France Insoumise, and Marine Le Pen, of the far-right National Front. To many, he looked like someone who understood the role of a free press in a modern democratic state.

The honeymoon did not last very long, and soon incidents marred the relationship.

The labour and culture ministers lodged complaints after newspapers Liberation and Le Monde published leaks about the government's reform plans.

The Elysée also incensed the media when it decided to select the journalists allowed to follow the head of state on foreign trips.

On 23 June 2017, media organisations, from L'Agence France-Presse to Le Monde, signed a joint letter starting with a blunt question: "Has the new executive a problem with press freedom?", and ending with a blunt statement. "Informing the public is as much a duty as a right. A free and independent press is essential to democracy."

In July, political columnist Denis Jeambar wrote a gently critical article which was meant as a warning: "Emmanuel Macron, in small brush strokes, puts the press under tension, maintains her at a distance, tries to discredit her, forgetting that the media's versatility and inconstancy served him well in the last three months of his campaign.

Macron, as Laurent Berger, leader of the centre-left trade union the French Democratic Confederation of Labour (CFDT), said in late April this year, "negates the role of intermediary institutions" such as unions or the media, adding that this was very dangerous.

"He is not a liberal," said Gaspard

Koening, director of the Génération Libre think-tank. "Neither in his understanding of individual freedoms nor in his conception of institutions: he is an umpteenth presidentialist, who adores the authoritarian structure of the Fifth Republic."

But for a number of public institutions, journalists are personae non gratae. This is not new, but representatives of the state feel free to impose a form of gagging law in the public space, especially during protests – a pattern confirmed by the Index-run Media Mapping Freedom Project showing numerous attempts by police and others to stop journalists covering French protests.

During the April rail strikes, TV crews were forbidden by the French train company SNCF to film and interview stranded passengers unless accompanied by a company "minder". The "correct" video footage was provided by the communications team. Likewise, during the evacuation of the Notre-Dame-des Landes squatters' camp (where a new airport had been planned) in early April, the gendarmerie closed the area to journalists and again provided its own videos to the media.

"We firmly condemn the practice of supplying, with the excuse of security, ready-made and sanitised images of undergoing 'sensitive' operations by the government," said the French National Union of Journalists (SNJ).

The Index-run Mapping Media Freedom project has also collected a worrying number of cases of reporters, especially photographers and cameramen, hit by stun grenades or tear gas canisters – and even beaten.

The new law grants wide-ranging powers to police and prefects while weakening judicial scrutiny over how those powers are used

"Since this government has decided to settle the social question with bludgeons, there is not one week without its case of journalists on the ground brutalised by police forces," said the SNJ.

France is now number 33 on Reporters without Borders' 2018 World Press Freedom Index, only slightly better than it was under Sarkozy and Hollande. The major issue remains the control exercised by corporate media owners, often very close to the state, on a large chunk of the most influential media.

But, "illiberal" clouds are hovering. There are worries about a bill on trade secrets (*secret des affaires*) which, they say, threaten whistleblowers and investigative journalism. By early May, the petition to block the law had gathered 550,000 signatures. The state of emergency, which was declared after the November 2015 terrorist attacks in Paris, was followed in November 2017 by a new anti-terror law "to strengthen internal security and the fight against terrorism", which integrated a number of its most controversial provisions.

Turning the exception into the "new normal" it was adopted over the objections of human rights groups, inter-governmental organisations, leading academics and even →

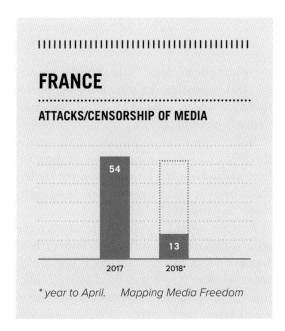

FRANCE

ATTACKS/CENSORSHIP OF MEDIA

54 — 2017
13 — 2018*

*year to April.   Mapping Media Freedom

→ of the domestic human rights oversight authority, who deemed it "liberticide". It was also criticised by the right and far-right, who denounced its "laxness".

The new law grants wide-ranging powers to police and prefects while weakening judicial scrutiny over how those powers are used. If it lifts the state of emergency prohibition of public demonstrations, restricting such measures to cases where "they threaten public order", it increases the prefects' powers to designate public spaces or events as "perimeters of protection" allowing the police to search people, bags and vehicles.

It also allows the police to search people without a warrant in a 20-kilometre radius of ports, airports and international train stations as well as close places of worship without prior judicial authorisation. The surveillance of electronic communications is also reinforced. Even if the law is meant to apply only "with the aim of preventing acts of terrorism", it is "a false exit from the state of emergency, a real backsliding of the rule

It is a false exit from the state of emergency, a real backsliding of the rule of law

of law", judged the French Human Rights League (LDH).

On 4 January, Macron, who was crudely targeted by disinformation during the 2017 presidential campaign, announced that a new law "on the trustworthiness of information" would be adopted before the next elections in order to promote increased internet transparency, fight fake news and foreign state-sponsored media disinformation.

"It would authorise a judge to block a website to stop the dissemination of what would be deemed fake news," Macron said.

"It could open a Pandora's box," Sylvain Rolland warned in La Tribune. The 1881

AHEAD OF THE GAME?

French thinkers came up with some of the early democratic ideas

1748: Montesquieu's On the Spirit of Laws is published. His view that government needs clearly defined separations of powers is instrumental in the American Revolution of 1776.

1762: Rousseau writes The Social Contract, which begins with the sentence: "Man is born free and everywhere he is in chains." The book helps inspire political reforms and revolutions in Europe and argues against the idea that monarchs are divinely empowered to legislate.

1789: The French Revolution begins, aimed at removing the monarchy and giving power to the people. The motto Liberté, égalité, fraternité emerges.

1789: The Declaration of the Rights of the Man and of the Citizen is published. Drafted by General Lafayette, Thomas Jefferson and Honoré Mirabeau, it has a major impact on the development of democracy worldwide

press law already bans "false news", it insisted. And entrusting the state with the power to decide what's news was not seen as a particularly good idea.

But the president's mistrust of the media threatens to feed the campaign of denigration which both the far right and the far left have been waging against the "establishment" or "liberal-left media".

Macron would do well to remember the wise words of his favorite philosopher Paul Ricoeur. "A democratic society is one which acknowledges that it is divided by contradictions of interests, and chooses to associate in equal terms each citizen in the expression, and inspires the 1948 United Nations Universal Declaration of Human Rights.

1804: Napoleon is crowned emperor of the First French Empire. The Napoleonic Code is created. Under this, male citizens are equal, inheritance laws are reformed and church is separated from state. The code becomes the main influence on the 19th century civil codes of most countries in Europe and Latin America.

1831: French sociologist and political theorist Alexis de Tocqueville travels to the USA and records his observations in Democracy in America (1835), one of the most influential books on equality and individualism from the 19th century.

1837: Charles Fourier, a French philosopher, is credited with coining the word "féminisme" to describe the emancipation he envisaged for women.

1848: The Second Republic rules France and the right to vote for all men, without any property qualifications, is established.

1944: Women in France gain the right to vote.

1962: The constitution is changed following a referendum so that the president is directly elected by the French people.

1968: Protests see students and workers across France call for more rights. While leading to no major legal changes at the time, established hierarchies are upended.

2000: The constitution is changed, with the maximum term a president can serve cut from seven years to five.

2015: Following terror attacks in Paris, a state of emergency is declared by President François Hollande. This grants the authorities exceptional powers to conduct searches for those believed linked to terrorism, with less judiciary oversight.

2017: President Emmanuel Macron ends the country's state of emergency. But he signs a counter-terrorism law that gives enforcement agencies greater authority to conduct searches, close religious facilities and limit the movements of those suspected of extremist links.

Jemimah Steinfeld

---

the analysis, the deliberation of these contradictions in order to arrive at an arbitration." The corollary is clear: a free and independent press matters.

Such commitment to press freedom is strategic for Macron. The far right has been striving to hijack the free speech banner, despite a history of physical attacks on, and legal actions against, journalists. On the internet, the fachosphere (the constellation of far right and national populist websites and twitter accounts) has been regularly slamming the president's alleged "will to muzzle freedom of expression".

In order to have more leverage at the European level, he must deprive those populist governments and illiberal parties who oppose his ambition to relaunch the European Union of any alibi.

"In the face of authoritarianism, the response is not authoritarian democracy but the authority of democracy," Macron said in his April speech to the European Parliament on 17 April in Strasbourg.

There is no other option than to lead by example. ⊗

Jean-Paul Marthoz is a veteran journalist, who writes regularly for Le Soir. He is a member of Index's editorial advisory board

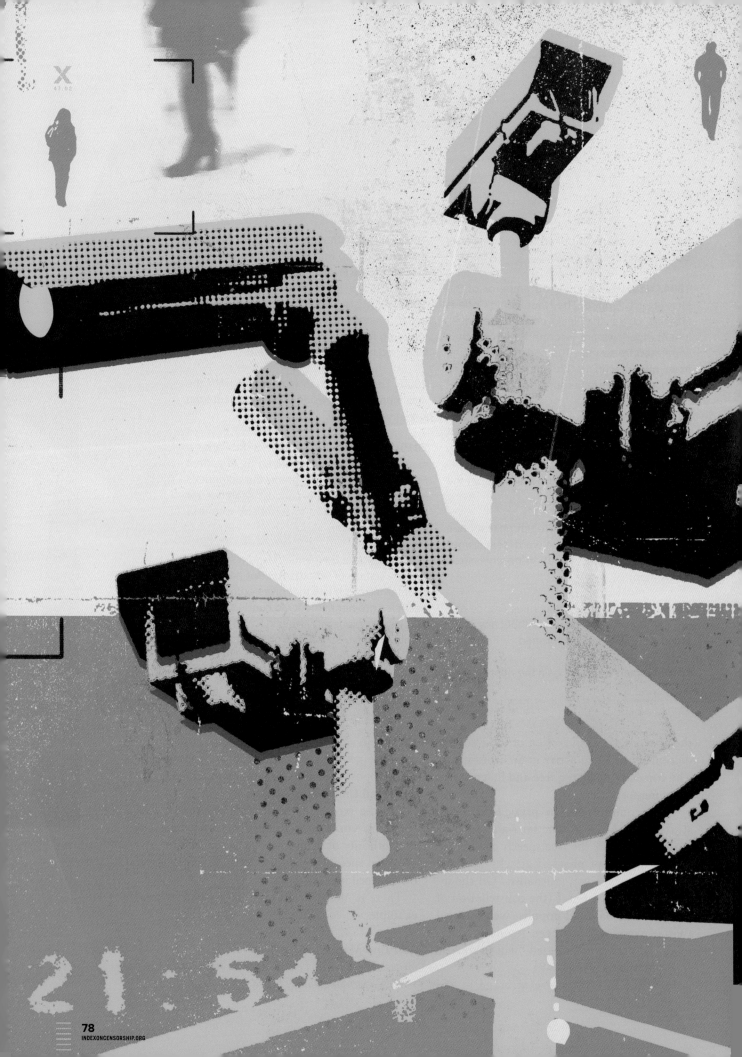

CULTURE

IN THIS SECTION

A walk in the park

47(02): 80/86 I DOI: 10.1177/0306422018784424

Sometimes a stroll is far more than it seems. In this new short story,
A Walk in the Park, by award-winning Turkish novelist **Kaya Genç** we
explore where it can end

IN YOUTH HE could only think about paradise. He imagined it as a field. There people lived in freedom and one could hear sounds of many flutes. He dreamt of entering that land inside his childhood bedroom and in the backseat of the family sedan. The land was Edenic, enticing and exciting. When he was seventeen, he read John Reed for the first time and he fell in love with the Russian revolution. That year he desired to travel to such earthly paradises as Soviet Russia. But his parents didn't share that desire. Neither did they share his affection for Ten Days that Shook the World.

For him paradise meant fireworks on streets, radicals lounging and discussing philosophy at cafes, and film crews experimenting with cinema in public squares and inside schools and ministries. Paradise meant women and men living in communes, their children not subject to laws of property or propriety, their hours spent not in offices but in nature. Paradise was long walks in the woods and a book waiting to be conquered at home.

But now he was an old man. He was bespectacled and he had a slight hunchback. He thought more about death and decay than paradise these days. His desire was to pass quickly and without much suffering to *jannah*, the final abode of Muslim believers.

Paradise was long walks in the woods and a book waiting to be conquered at home

He didn't believe in an earthly paradise any longer. In his forties he annoyed his friends when his politics shifted from Marxist to Islamist. As he walked on the pathway of Paradise Park he was suddenly reminded of those days of conversion. If it was not for the name of the park he would perhaps be pondering other things: his back pains or the cat he was planning to get for his grandson. Tarik had another hour in practice, and he liked wandering the neighbourhood while waiting for the young athlete to emerge from the doors of the tennis club.

This was not the sort of wandering he did in his Reed-reading days. Back then he used to walk in poor neighbourhoods and avoid those streets inhabited by Turkish toffs. He spent his youthful days marching under banners and shoulder to shoulder with the working class. He shouted slogans about the ownership of the means of production. But this afternoon he only walked to kill time.

That morning, in the cab, the name of Riza, his old comrade, came up on the radio. He learned that poor Riza had died of a heart attack after supper last night. That was an unexpected end for a man he anticipated dying in a Turkish torture chamber when they were young. Turkey's paternalistic state severely punished pursuers of para-   dises.   Still   they   both survived those perilous days. Riza, in his forties, became a professor of sociology and he lectured on utopias and Marxism at the city's premier university of social sciences. He was considered a leading defender of lost causes. From the tone of the radio broadcast it seemed as if his funeral the next morning would be well-attended.

People admired Riza because he insisted on what he believed in. He never changed ideological tracks. He appeared certain that death equalled nothingness and it was nothing to worry about. His life had been a struggle to reach that place Marx describes in The German Ideology: "there one hunts in the morning, fishes in the afternoon, rears cattle in the evening, criticises after dinner without ever becoming hunter, fisherman, herdsman or critic." Riza was a versatile man. He excited and inspired people around him. Women talked about living in the paradise of his company.

He did not, of course, cry when news of his death landed so unexpectedly inside the cab. But his face must have revealed some sign of devastation. Tarik had suddenly asked him about Riza and their friendship. All he could come up with was a mumbling he was a good man and a faltering he must have gone to paradise.

That was an unexpected end for a man he anticipated dying in a Turkish torture chamber when they were young

---

✳

SWANS STIRRED ON the lake and a guard patrolled the Edenic scene. Apparently elderly men and women have been coming to the lake to end their lives. After nocturnal wanderings cancer patients filled their lungs with the lake's dark waters. Alzheimer's patients, confused about swimming, watched its dark surface as waves immersed them inside the lake's black depths.

The guard's uniform was also black, the colour of death. For a moment he considered asking the guard's name and age. He could even inquire about his family. He had sustained a lifelong curiosity about the lives of strangers. "Help from God," he mumbled: in Hebrew the name of Azrael, the angel of death, translated to "Help from God". He wondered what Riza would have asked the guard if his heart hadn't stopped beating. What had Azrael told Riza himself last night?

Over the 1970s, they had been fascistic in their pursuit of a communist state. They passionately   fought superstitions and religious dogma. They believed in giving up earthly pleas-   ures to reach a Marxist paradise. Riza was cheerful about this tactic. →

→ As they wandered the college gardens a few months before the military coup in 1980, he instructed him to enjoy the hard labour of bringing about paradise on earth. That task, he said, demanded dedication, devotion and discipline.

The silent swans started moving on the matt lake and he thought of Tarik who would no doubt have enjoyed watching them. For the fatherless child, the appearances become a consolation.

After his father's death last year, Tarik had become much attached to animals. But in January, after visiting a zoo, he had googled the history of the institution. He learned about the Animal Liberation Front. During breakfast the following morning, he announced his intention to liberate their pet cat. She was given permission to roam the garden. But as dusk fell that evening the cat disappeared. She was never seen again. Tarik cried when he heard the news. There was a highway nearby and cars rarely slowed down at night. To console him he told his grandson there was no paradise on this earth. He instructed him to never believe again anyone who told him otherwise. Nature was violent, cities were unpredictable, and this was the best of all possible worlds. He should have kept the cat inside.

Swans stirred on the lake and a guard patrolled the Edenic scene. Apparently elderly men and women have been coming to the lake to end their lives

The guard appeared thoughtful as he lit a cigarette. His head seemed crushed beneath invisible concerns. He was the kind of man they dreamed of saving in their youth. But he was also the kind of man who resisted their promises of an earthly paradise. Men like him listened to what they had to say, and then talked about *şükretmek*, a state of gratitude to Allah. They believed in a future filled with better things to come. That future was designed by the All-Powerful and All-Knowing Ruler of the Universe.

Of course Riza would tell them about the illusionary nature of *şükretmek* and the irrational source of belief in gods. He described those as symptoms of what Marx called false consciousness. But Turks preferred *şükretmek* and *jannah* to Marx's *falsches Bewußtsein*, and they insisted on waiting for Allah's gardens of paradise rather than perishing inside Turkey's jails of hell.

In his forties, he would tell that story to his son to explain his conversion to Islam. It was what the Turkish working class wanted, he told his son. He tried to explain his logic for exchang-   ing a Marxist paradise with an Islamic one. "I wanted to participate in their dreams   and beliefs. I wanted to better understand their destitution."

He couldn't survive the loss of his son, who joined an armed group and died in a street fight in a foreign city across the Syrian border, if he didn't believe he was going to a better place.

He noticed that the guard's upper lip was twitching. He assumed it was about poverty. It could as well have been adultery. He didn't have the means to know. He got up and walked away, disappearing behind the shrubs to allow the man his privacy.

Still he wanted to hear the guard's inner voice. He wondered if he was talking to Allah at the moment. Who would save the poor man from his misery, if not for Allah? People were all desperate. There was no glimmer of hope for the fallen. A cloud covered the sun. Darkness entered the Paradise Park.

He walked past a rose tree. He wondered if Riza would walk to the guard to ask about his worries. Perhaps he would attempt to see if something could be done to relieve his pains. He, on the other hand, chose to leave all that to Allah. His son, he believed, was looked after in *jannah*. He had to believe in that. Belief is the only saviour.

*

Who would save the poor man from his misery, if not for Allah? People were all desperate. There was no glimmer of hope for the fallen

A WOODEN HUT appeared in the northern side of the park. It was ivy-covered and he didn't at first notice its presence. It was that that then intrigued him. The air inside the hut was damp. There was a chair at its centre. It was surrounded by cigarette butts and a matchbox. But he preferred to stand.

This was what many working class houses used to feel like when he visited them with Riza during their college years. They called those "missionary visits". They would receive the addresses of worker apartments from unions. At the entrance they would always be greeted by a headscarved woman. She would tell them "*As-salāmu 'alaykum.*" They would reply: "Hello, comrade, thanks for allowing us inside."

The houses often smelt of cabbage. He would be unsettled by the way workers had learned to live in poverty and ugliness. Still they believed in a better world to come. It was, perhaps, the idea of the unattainability of that better world to come that led him to change his direction. But he was a bit worried. There was much power in *şükretmek*, but it was also a weakness if it made him blind to the suffering of the world around him. He shouldn't have let him go to Syria.

→ He heard a voice from outside. "Sir, this hut is closed to the public."

It was the guard. Perhaps he came there to smoke in private. He should have guessed that it was his refuge: the guard's own little paradise.

"It used to be called the Paradise Hut," the voice said. "Some believe they used to get in touch with ghosts of loved ones here."

"Who did?"

"Those who came here fifty years ago," the guard said.

"How about cats?" he said.

"What about them?"

"I want to get one for my grandson."

There was a pause. A moment passed in silent consideration. The guard said there was an orange-coloured cat a few meters near the Paradise Hut. She was born two months ago. She had good manners. She had a funny purr.

"If you get the cat it will be *sawāb* [a spiritual reward] for me," the guard said. "Mohammad, peace be upon him, would rather cut out his robe than to wake a cat, as you well know Sir."

They waited for its new guests, those destined to consider life and those who prepared to die

---

He checked his watch and noticed it was past six o'clock.

The guard was now outside the hut. He imagined the silent flow of swans who watched the calm of the park. They waited for its new guests, those destined to consider life and those who prepared to die. He thought of his son. The doctors said he was shot in the heart.

He noticed he was already late for Tarik. It would take him fifteen minutes to reach the gates. Once at the gates he would tell his grandson about the orange-coloured cat. That would cheer him up. He would tell him about Riza and the 1970s. He was a good man. He must have gone to paradise. He would ask for forgiveness from his son, and from Riza. He would beg for forgiveness from all those whose earthly paradises he failed to notice. ⊗

Kaya Genç is an author of numerous fiction and non-fiction books. He is based in Istanbul and is also Index on Censorship's contributing editor for Turkey

Georgian plain speaking

47(02): 87/94 | DOI: 10.1177/0306422018784425

Novelist and playwright **Lasha Bugadze** talks to **Rachael Jolley** about controversies surrounding his writing and why he feels positive about the future in Georgia. Plus we translate an extract from his new novel

LASHA BUGADZE uses satire at the heart of his writing, which he said is a very Georgian trait.

"I started writing absurd genre plays. Sometimes absurd is very logical for Georgians," said the author, whose play The President Has Come To See You was performed at London's Royal Court, as well as theatres around the world. He also wrote the satirical play Putin's Mum about the mysterious Vera Putina, a Georgian woman who, since 1999, has claimed Russian President Vladimir Putin is her lost son.

Bugadze said his first creative foray was via cartoons. He began drawing in his childhood, when Georgia was still part of the Soviet Union, to take issue with the controlling regime. From cartoons he went on to experiment with other styles of writing.

"My first play was performed in 1998, when I was 20 years old," he said. "My first novel was published in 2005. Writing became my profession."

As an artist, he is no stranger to controversy and knows what it is like to feel the establishment rallying against him. It did so when he published his satirical tale The First Russian, which played with a storyline about the relationship of the 12th and 13th century Queen Tamar of Georgia and her Russian husband.

"My small satirical novel became very scandalous. Some parliament members believed that I had insulted Georgian history and Queen Tamar. Orthodox members of the patriarchate (the office of the Georgian church) were outraged. Some of them called for me to be banished."

One of the themes in his new novel, Little Country, of which we publish an excerpt below, is the power of religion.

"In the Soviet times, religion was repressed, then [after Soviet times] the church gained influence on society and [it] became a state within the state," he said. "My novel is about this... It is about hate of love, competition for power and populism."

Today he feels optimistic about the environment for writers in Georgia, despite the possibility of the introduction of a new blasphemy law that could lead to prosecution for offending religious feelings.

His novel, with its consideration of recent Georgian censorship, has been published by a Georgian publisher. "Georgia is a democratic country and we have freedom of speech. Fortunately, it's a very fundamental right for Georgians," said Bugadze. →

ABOVE: Georgian author Lasha Bugadze

→ That said, he added, "Sure, society is [more] open now than before, for example 18 years ago, but we still face lots of challenges, and the main challenge is Russia and the danger coming from Russia."

The five-day invasion of 2008 is still in his mind and, speaking to Bugadze, while he no longer lives under the watchful eyes of the Soviet Union, he worries that Russia still exerts its influence in the country, through politics and the media. Perhaps material for his next piece of work, whatever form it may take. ⊗

Rachael Jolley is the editor of Index on Censorship magazine

Little Country

BY LASHA BUGADZE

THE CATHOLICOS-PATRIARCH OF Georgia was sitting far from us in a low, gilded armchair under a chandelier which seemed almost to touch the floor.

Georgia's history was staring at us from a gigantic modern fresco: life-size figures, churches and monasteries and the easily recognisable Georgian glaciers.

It seemed as if a gigantic chorus, consisting of saints, kings and queens, was waiting for us, together with the Patriarch. The grim faces, depicted realistically by a modern artist, were looking fixedly at us with identical expressions so that you felt they were all twins, or pictures of the artist himself who, wittingly or unwittingly, had made everybody look like himself.

The saintly kings and queens had healthy, proud faces; some of them, those who stood a little lower with their arms crossed as tradition dictates, had their round faces and double chins lit up by thick candles stuck into tall candle holders. Above them, the golden crowns of the second rank of kings shone in the light of the chandelier. Somewhere in the middle stood David IV 'The Builder', holding Gelati church in his hand, while next to him was a copy of another ancient fresco – the three-metre high Queen Tamar from Vardzia, holding out her hands in imprecation to a gigantic George III.

From where I was standing I could see, behind everybody else, the shadowy angry face of one of the kings, possibly Bagrat III. In any case, I looked for a while at Bagrat staring from the murk, at his kitschy-realistic grim face, and finally at the living contrast to this fresco, the smiling Patriarch whose head was just slightly inclined to the right.

A familiar smile, which I had become used to as a child and which was now part of me.

I wondered, should I kneel down?

No sooner had I approached than I bent triple.

I had the illusion that someone was whispering to me: "Kiss his hand!"

The Patriarch's hand quivered slightly.

Suddenly I remembered that I had been told by someone that the Patriarch, when he didn't wish his hand to be kissed by someone bent over him, withdrew his wrist into the sleeve of his surplice: you bent down and the hand vanished. He didn't want to be kissed, and that was the end of the matter.

I poked my face somewhere between his sleeve and his wrist.

"Aha, our troublemaker-in-chief has come," said the Patriarch, and smiled his familiar smile again.

The fresco went dark. So did the grim, swarthy Bagrat III, and all the others looking at us from the wall. It was now that I saw three priests or monks in black surplices standing behind the Patriarch's armchair: among them, as I found out later, was His Holiness Kristepore; on the left of the armchair was Father Tadeos, Koba, who commented on the text of two announcements from the time when I had first visited, and the secretary Khatuna, who was holding The Epoch of Freedom, which I thought I had left in the reception room but was now here.

There was a television in one corner of the hall, and you could hear a stage song coming from it: an unlit Andrea Bocelli was singing on television.

We sat down in two low armchairs.

The Patriarch watched me with a bewildered smile, his slightly open mouth and apparently out-turned thick lower lip made his face seem even more bewildered.

"How are you?" I heard him ask very quietly: in fact the sound was made by his moving lips, not his voice; and I realised that I had to be very alert if I was going to catch his words.

"We're worried, Your Holiness," My Father replied, even more quietly, with exaggerated humility.

The Patriarch did not respond; he adjusted his spectacles with trembling hands and turned barely perceptibly to his secretary.

"Is he here?"

"Yes indeed, Your Holiness," she nodded to him.

"Come closer," the Patriarch told me.

"Go up closer," the others whispered to me: they repeated his every word like an echo.

I went up as close as I could (my big armchair seemed to me to be nailed to the floor).

The secretary laid a magazine that had been opened, probably deliberately, at a specific page on the Patriarch's lap; the old man once again adjusted his silver-framed spectacles, which were slipping down his nose, and followed the words with a trembling finger.

"Explain it to us, would you?" He gave me a sidelong glance, as if his neck hurt and he had trouble straightening his head up.

I looked at the magazine: a few sentences were underlined in red.

"What have you written here?"

The secretary bent down again, picked up the magazine cautiously and somewhat awkwardly, as if picking up a magazine demanded a certain amount of effort from her, and then called on me.

→

→   "Read it," the others urged me. I looked up at the Patriarch. His face was bewildered, his mouth half-open, and he was looking at me as before.

"Read it," I heard behind me.

"Which bit? The bit underlined in red?" I tried to smile, but I managed to look up, encountered the faces of the angry Bagrat III or Bagrat IV, and looked down at the magazine again.

"Yes," Khatuna told me.

I read: "Now let us say, Our Father…"

I didn't know whether I should have read it again or not. Or why I should read it. I felt as if I was taking an examination.

I fell silent.

Suddenly the Patriarch spoke up again, more quietly than the silence around him:

"Why do you make fun of that prayer? We say Our Father every day, don't we?"

He spoke with such a sense of grievance and so sadly that I was suddenly terribly worried. I felt embarrassed – not by what I had written but by him, an old and kindly man whom I had unwittingly offended.

"Why do I make fun of it?" I repeated his question like a pupil, and I looked at My Father. Perhaps it was better if he answered instead of me. No, it turned out that I was the one who had to answer all the questions (or I was induced to do so)…

"I'm not making fun of it, I myself say Our Father every day, Your Holiness."

I said "Your Holiness" and I was amazed, because my own voice sounded alien to me.

Couldn't someone have switched off the television sound? It occurred to me that here they did this on purpose, to block out speech. Someone told me that when the security services are listening in, you should have everything turned up loud: the radio, the television, music… This Patriarch had always been listened in on. Probably even now the Patriarch was aware of it and that was why nobody switched off the television. Maybe that was now a tradition. Complete silence was forbidden in his office.

 "It's our prayer," he continued gravely, but sweetly, each syllable distinct. "It is a powerful prayer."

The old man adjusted his spectacles (which had not slipped down, but which he probably thought had slipped) with the same gravity and caution, and looked at my magazine.

"What is this supposed to be?"

"Oh dear," I thought. "If we've sunk to the point where Yuri the Russian has sex with a broody hen, things are going to be very awkward."

Khatuna stood next to me and, apparently, began looking for the extract she needed. It may have been her who had been wielding the red pen.

Once again I glanced at My Father and at Dato the First. I hoped I had really convinced him and removed the irritating episodes.

Further down, a phrase where I described the Georgian monarch's backside had been →

→ underlined in red. Why had I written that idiotic sentence! No, there was no way I could read it out now…

"You read it," I asked Khatuna. "I'm embarrassed to do so in His Holiness's presence."

My Father, Dato the First and Father Tadeos laughed quietly, sympathetically, with a desire to support me.

"Then why did you write such a thing? Aren't we a beautiful people?" the Patriarch said, looking up at me.

He knew what it was that I couldn't read out. All the same, did I have to describe the physical attributes of Georgian women in the presence of his Holiness and His Blessedness? No, Your Holiness, everyone has the same backside – sport and a healthy diet do the job.

"Queen Tamar was beautiful," the Patriarch continued. "Why did you write like that? Many people have been offended. Shouldn't a writer see the beautiful in a human being? Especially in such a glorious monarch…"

He had an odd way, obscure and sugary, of pronouncing his 'shs…

It was strange: an elderly Patriarch was defending Georgian genes from me. It was as if in his person Georgia was defending the physical and spiritual attributes of Georgians.

I didn't know what I should do. Should I have apologised? If only someone would come to my aid. How, and on what grounds should I be debating with an elderly Patriarch talking to me about the beauty of a 13th century queen?

"Her eyebrows were joined together, as in the fresco," the secretary read out.

"Which fresco shows they were joined together? The Gelati or the Vardzia ones?" the Patriarch asked with the same amazement. "They're not joined on our fresco," he smiled. "You should have looked first and then written."

A young, energetic woman was looking out at us from the fresco: a neo-Georgian copy of the Vardzia Queen Tamar.

"She has remarkable eyebrows, remarkable," whispered My Father, who had decided to help me. "They're very artistic."

"It's your fault, Giorgi," the Patriarch turned towards him. "You should have taught him properly."

On television a folk ensemble had begun dancing.

I looked behind me. A bodyguard was standing by the television.

My Father instantly blushed. Because he felt insulted, not because he was embarrassed by the Patriarch, not because he was worried about me, but by a feeling of superiority; he wanted to say something with emphatic arrogance, because, in principle, he didn't consider the Patriarch to be any sort of authority, even though, obviously, he was sitting there quietly and, his face bright red, listening to a rebuke.

"There was something else," Khatuna said, and bent over my head like a schoolteacher. She pointed out a particular paragraph with her finger and whispered with a smile, "Here…"

The Patriarch couldn't grasp what his secretary meant, so Khatuna reverently, with the same fixed smile, but with more precision, commented again:

"The chapters are numbered backwards, so you have to leaf through the pages backwards, and that has upset some people."

The old man, his head leaning to one side, looked at me expectantly. I could see curiosity in his eyes.

I think they were very bored and were amusing themselves with me.

I bent my head in exactly the same way as he had, because I thought for some reason that he would understand my words better if I wasn't sitting upright.

"It's a literary game," I said. "It's a post-modern text."

The word "post-modern" sounded in this hall as if I had belched or pronounced an obscenity out loud.

The face of the bushy-bearded Sanctity (probably Kristepore) standing behind the Patriarch expressed reproach: he looked just like the figures on the fresco.

"These -isms are terrible," said the Patriarch.

We have to talk about this, young people don't know about it. All evil begins with mockery

"He means the modern trends in culture, Your Holiness," My Father spoke up in my defence.

"That was how the communists used to persecute us," the old man looked at him. "Our clergy and our churches and monasteries suffered very badly because of them. They swore at the priests and mocked the Christian saints. We have to talk about this, young people don't know about it. All evil begins with mockery. First, people express contempt for things, then they get the people used to the idea that the holy and the valuable are nothing, and finally they moved to destroying the clergy and the pure at heart."

Those standing behind him expressed agreement silently by synchronised nods of their heads. The dozens of saints on the fresco confirmed the truth of what the old man was saying.

Father Tadeos was looking at me as if these words were coming from his lips, not from the Patriarch's.

"Yes indeed, I know, Your Holiness," I said quietly, although I badly wanted the time to come to make my own complaints and to talk about the people, the unidentified persons and the legendary thugs from Akhaltsikhe camping outside my house in support of the Patriarch. Ever since childhood I had listened to these stories of priests tortured and shot by the Bolsheviks, and in particular about one priest who had been shot in 1983 for hijacking an aeroplane and who had, unlike my godparent, not actually been on the plane… →

→   "Such thoughts are bad," said the Patriarch, looking at those sitting next to me. He looked at them for a short while, as if he expected a response from them, then he turned to me. "What did you have in mind? Why did you write about Queen Tamar?"

Why had I written? What the hell, I didn't know. Did my answer affect anything? I felt again almost as awkward as I had a long time before when my grandfather tried to find out the bad word which a football trainer had said to me. Actually, why did the queen have such an unsportsmanlike body? But what sort of body should she have had? Long legs and a narrow waist? Would that sort of joke be allowable?

"He's a very patriotic lad, Your Holiness," My Father suddenly joined in. "There is a sort of misunderstanding, when someone shouts out loud to us that they are to be considered patriots: actually, they are chauvinists. There's no difference. I remember, once the school was given a day off on 26 May and it was the birthday of one of the pupils and they spent all their money on a taxi and went all round town with flags of the First Republic… It was 1988, or 1989 and they were just children, that was a different generation…"

This story made no impression on the old man. He couldn't sense in the slightest what we had experienced or how, and he wasn't interested in what I was frightened of or whether anyone was really threatening me. He was somewhat distant, cold in fact, and he seemed to be expecting us to say, do or become something else, so that this evening would be memorable not just because of what was on the television.

Why had I written it? I was expected to answer.

The Patriarch's head drooped as if he was plunged in thought or had gone to sleep.

"Tomorrow there is a session of the Synod," Father Tadeos, who was standing behind him in the darkness, said in a low, but assured and succinct voice. (It was too dark for his face to be visible, so that one had the impression that one of the kings or queens on the fresco had spoken.) "People are upset. You have to make a public apology for your story, or you will have to answer to the irate parishioners."

For some reason I thought that this was a point when only the Patriarch should have spoken and I was almost astounded when I heard Father Tadeos's voice.

"Yes," the Patriarch agreed quietly, and lifted his spectacles.

And I suddenly realised, or rather it was revealed to me, that if anyone was expecting something, it wasn't my response, my penitence or my apology, but the Patriarch's questions and firmness.

Now they were looking at him, not at me.

Translated by **Donald Rayfield**

Lasha Bugadze *is an award-winning Georgian novelist, playwright and presenter. His play The President Has Come To See You was performed at London's Royal Court*

Little big voice

47(02): 95/97 | DOI: 10.1177/0306422018784427

Dubbed Vietnam's Lady Gaga, **Mai Khoi** talks to **Jemimah Steinfeld** about having her house raided and reaction to her lyrics

"**THOUGH SHE BE** but little, she is fierce," said Helena in Shakespeare's A Midsummer Night's Dream. The same could be said of Mai Khoi, the singer-turned-activist, who is currently one of the biggest thorns in the side of the Vietnamese government.

Over WhatsApp instant messenger (we try to speak but, mysteriously, our phones won't connect), Khoi outlines the abuse she has suffered at its hands. She says she has been blocked from Facebook and evicted from her house, and her shows have been raided. In March, she was detained at the airport in Hanoi for eight hours following her album tour of Europe.

"They asked so many questions which were very private, and they took all of my CDs and books that my friends gave me," she said. Today, she is scared.

"They have secret police everywhere to know where I go, what I do … I always look around before I go out of my place."

Vietnam is at a crossroads. The Communist Party of Vietnam, which has been fully in power since 1976, presides over an increasingly wealthy, young and tech-savvy nation, which hankers for greater rights.

At the same time, the government is hellbent on more control, even following China's lead in certain areas. "The [draft] Vietnamese Cyber Security law, which will restrict freedom of speech, was almost copied from the Chinese cyber security law," Khoi said.

And she is not willing to look the other way.

"People in my country really need freedom of expression," she said.

"As an artist, I don't feel free to create under the censorship system and that's why I want to protect and promote freedom of expression. I don't agree with the unequal and dictatorial ideas.

"People have been in jail if they sang love songs in the past. Now, no one goes to jail because of singing love songs anymore, but if we sing about politics and human rights we will be in trouble.

"What is freedom of expression? People in my country, even many activists, don't understand what's freedom of expression. When I protested [against Donald] Trump, many activists were saying that what I did was not freedom of expression."

Khoi refers to last November, when the US president visited her country. She walked through the streets with a banner reading "Piss on you Trump".

"Trump has demonstrated that he doesn't care about human rights and does not recognise civil society in Vietnam," she said. "He also wants to send refugees back to Vietnam. This would be terrible for those people and against the Geneva Convention. However, the human rights situation in Vietnam →

LEFT: The singer Mai Khoi, who uses her music and platform to call for more democracy in Vietnam

They have secret police everywhere to know where I go, what I do ... I always look around before I go out of my place

was getting worse before Trump was elected and we can't blame him for all of our problems. But, for sure, he is not helping."

Khoi shot to fame in 2010 when she won the Vietnam Television Song and Album of the Year Award, the biggest accolade for songwriting in the country. She revealed her rebellious streak early on: almost immediately after her win, she shaved off half her hair and inscribed the letters VN, for Vietnam, on one side of her head, a move that

was harshly criticised by the country's conservative media. Since then she's constantly spoken out about sexuality, LGBT rights and violence against women.

In 2016, she became the first Vietnamese celebrity to nominate herself for the National Assembly, Vietnam's legislative body, on a pro-democracy platform. (She also met then US President Barack Obama and the two discussed human rights in the country.)

Since running for parliament, she has effectively been banned from singing in Vietnam, so her concerts are all private performances. Despite this, Khoi remains upbeat. She tells me she's "happy and very proud" to be the first Vietnamese musician to release an album with an international record label.

CREDIT: Bennett Murray

Please, sir

Please, sir,
Let us give you money so
    you'd allow us to work,
Please, sir,
Let us be treacherous like
    you, so you'd allow us to
    be as stupid as you,
Please, sir,
Will you let us sing?
Let us put up the paintings
    to admire them,
Will you let us love?
Let us bend down, begging you
    for savagery and cruelty,
Please, sir,
Let us publish books,
Let us move freely,
Let us protect the nation,
Please, sir,
Let us share information,
Allow us to do charitable work,
Give us our constitutional rights,
Our constitutional rights,
Our constitutional rights.

LEFT: Mai Khoi protesting against Trump's visit to Vietnam in November 2017

Khoi is frequently likened to strong, female singers including Lady Gaga, Madonna and Pussy Riot, but it feels almost reductive to make comparisons. Her work is, instead, a unique product of Vietnam. She describes the style of the new album with her band Mai Khoi Chem Gio as "ethnic meets free jazz" and explains how it "has captured all of the emotions and challenges" that her band have faced in recent years, including one show that was raided by 40 police.

The song published above, translated into English for the first time, comes from the band's new album, Dissent. Entitled Please Sir, it's "about how we have to ask for permission to sing, exhibit art and exercise many other basic rights".

When it comes to her country's future,

Khoi has tempered optimism. "I always think in an optimistic way. Thinking positively makes me have more energy to create. I will see how my country's situation will change in the next election," she said.

"Many people in Vietnam understand politics as something that politicians do. They say they don't care about politics because they don't see how everything around them is political. But now people are more engaged because they have access to more information now than before and they can think more critically. Social media also means that people can interact and organise in ways they could not before." ✖

Jemimah Steinfeld is deputy editor of Index on Censorship magazine

Facing the future

47(02): 98/102 I DOI: 10.1177/0306422018784426

Award-winning short story writer **Jonathan Tel** introduces his new work of fiction, and tells **Danyaal Yasin** what inspired it

CREDIT: Marco Jeurissen/Ikon

"**F**ACIAL RECOGNITION TECHNOLOGY is something to be seriously concerned about around the world, including in the UK," said author Jonathan Tel ahead of the release of his new short story, 2084.

The technology has been in the international news lately – Facebook is currently seeking consent to use recognition software in Europe, which is already in use in other parts of the world – and Tel, the winner of the Sunday Times 2016 short story prize, has explored this issue as a jumping-off point for his new piece of fiction, published exclusively in this issue.

His story creates a society where appearance dictates everything, including the type of food you eat and how much toilet roll you receive, something already implemented in China, where one public toilet in Beijing dispenses paper using facial recognition software.

However, the Chinese state has less control than some people might think, Tel said. "China is actually a more chaotic society than perhaps the government wishes it were. They certainly tend to project this idea that it's a unified society, but it's chaotic and the government doesn't control things that much.

"What I'm not trying to do with the story is specifically criticise what's going on now. I would rather deal with what the dangers might be in the future. The danger could be that it could lead to some sort of Orwellian-type situation in which people are controlled too much.

"When Orwell wrote 1984, he didn't seriously think Britain was going to become like 1984, but he thought it might move in that direction and it's a way of talking about the things that citizens were concerned about. Same with my story. I don't know which way it's going because I don't know the future, but it's there as a sort of parable."

Exploring the dark turns that could exist in a potentially government-controlled future, Tel uses the real-life scenarios occurring in countries such as China to create a seemingly unified society. The dystopia →

created by Tel takes a dark turn when the protagonist runs into an attractive woman, one he will do anything to impress. Tel said: "I describe a society in which the government is trying to achieve authoritarian control. That indeed is to be feared, as Orwell pointed out. But in my story, the government partially fails, and the attempt results in a society riddled with corruption and injustice and petty revenge, which is also to be feared." ⊗

Danyaal Yasin is the editorial assistant at Index on Censorship

2084

A FANFARE FROM his phone, and Pine wakes up. He levers himself upright, and peers into the mirror. He's unshaven, bleary-eyed, tottering. He picks up his phone, which displays an image of his face altered to make him seem better looking than in reality. The phone greets him by name. "Congratulations! You are in the 98th percentile of handsomeness! As a reward, you may enter a sweepstake to win a fabulous prize!" He types in his name and ID, but when it comes to entering his birth date for some reason the System refuses to accept he was born in 1984. "Illegal number!" it says, and autocorrects this to 2084. A bug in the System, he guesses, as happens often enough.

Whereas Pine is tired, the version of himself on his phone is alert and energetic. He stares wistfully at this new and improved model.

The man emerges from his windowless room in the housing complex in the exurb of a third-tier city. It is not yet dawn. He is funnelled through to a commuter bus. The System recognises his face and greets him by name, assigning him a seat.

Three hours later, he arrives in an office tower by the fourth ring road. The System identifies him; doors slide open and an elevator takes him to the correct level. Illuminated arrows direct him to the cubicle where he is to work today. The government has installed an automated nationwide System which recognises everyone and keeps track of their behaviour, in theory. What matters is that the government gives the illusion of being in control, whether or not it actually is. In practice, the algorithm often fails, and has to be supplemented by the input of humans, such as him. His job is to recognise faces. He compares a photo from a security camera with one in an ID. The same person: yes or no? Swipe right or swipe left? The task is gamified. He wins virtual prizes and rises to higher levels as he works. It's like playing a rather boring computer game.

The System decides when it is time for his lunch break. He accompanies two co-workers – Plum, who is on the fat side, and Bamboo, who is skinny. The System sends them to a fast-food chicken restaurant. On entry, the System scans their appearance and decides what they would surely like to order. Pine gets a bowl of rice porridge with preserved egg; Plum a double-order of thighs and fries; and Bamboo a single drumstick. Plum grumbles how the

System is expanding his waistline. The three men go to the toilet. The toilet paper dispenser issues three sheets per person. When Bamboo presses the button for more, a message flashes up that he's already received his allowance; he contorts his face, sucking in his cheeks and dilating his nostrils, so he passes for a different person, and is granted three more sheets. All around the room, men in need of extra toilet paper are puffing up their cheeks, sticking out their tongues, making duck lips, winking and blinking, rolling their eyes, squinting and gurning and metamorphosing their faces in every conceivable manner – successfully or not.

Just as the co-workers are exiting the restaurant, a man is trying to enter. He is dishevelled, stubbled, with panda eyes, and is mumbling something about how he's a victim of mistaken identity and seeks justice. He looks oddly familiar. The transparent doors slam shut, blocking the malcontent. Pine sees urban security personnel wearing their informational sunglasses striding forward. A woman stands in the entryway, keeping the doors open, allowing the man to pass by her and elude the Sunglasses. He disappears among the diners. Her behaviour is ambiguous: it's not clear whether or not she is helping the malcontent intentionally, though Pine suspects the worst. There's something queerly attractive about her soft-heartedness, and he's drawn to her appearance, too... Pine decides he's fallen in love.

Back at the office he consults the database. Might the System please tell him the name of the woman? It will, on condition he supplies information on an anti-social act. He confirms that Plum vociferously objected to his meal. And might the System also tell him the woman's tastes, habits and how he might meet her? Pine learns all this, in return for revealing Bamboo's theft of toilet paper.

The following day, Plum and Bamboo are not at work. Pine reckons they've been sent to Re-education for a stretch. For their own good, surely: Plum will lose weight and Bamboo will learn to follow the rules. It's not as if his betrayal could cause them serious harm – they won't be put in a room full of rats, or anything. As the proverb goes: In calamity lies fortune, in fortune lies calamity.

After work, he hurries to be standing at a particular intersection at a particular time. He is carrying a stack of papers. A female commuter can't help knocking into him. He drops his papers. She apologises. "Not at all," he says. This is the woman, though it's funny how she looks different in the open air. They introduce themselves. "My friends call me Pine," he says. She says: "And mine, Jujube." He invites her to join him for a bowl of fermented mung bean soup and a snack of grilled pork tongue – dishes she is particularly fond of, according to the System.

He slurps the sour murky soup, while she hardly sips hers. "We have so much in common!" he assures her. The grilled tongue is brought out. She comments: "That pig must have said something bad in a previous life." He tells her his favourite colour is blue – just as hers is, or so the System informed him. Normally he is shy with women, but now he is confident. He examines his own idyllic image on his phone. Congratulations! You are in the 99th →

→ percentile of handsomeness! Jujube agrees to meet him the following week.

They date regularly, and become lovers. For their first anniversary, he suggests a dinner at the chicken restaurant where he'd first seen her. She remarks she's never been there before. "But surely…" he says. "And besides, you do like mung bean soup and pork tongue, don't you, and blue is your favourite colour?" She tells him she doesn't care for the soup or the meat, and prefers yellow. He realises the System misinformed him: she wasn't the woman who helped the malcontent. No matter, Jujube will do as a girlfriend. Any lover is better than none at all, and he guesses she feels the same way about him. He sneezes. She says: "A sneeze means people are talking about you behind your back." They agree to meet at the restaurant the following day for lunch.

That morning before work, he goes to the toilet where he encounters Bamboo, who is washing his hands with the precise allocated amount of soap. He's just been released from the Re-education facility. In the corridor he runs into Plum, thinner than before, who blurts unprompted: "I love the System."

"And the System loves you," says Pine. The worst possible government he can conceive of is chaos, and the System promises, at least, freedom from that.

Pine is not feeling well. He has a cough and earache, his eyes are sore and rheumy. He rushes, but gets to the restaurant a little late. As he approaches, he waves to Jujube who is waiting for him just inside. But when he approaches the entrance, the doors slide shut, blocking him. A warning light goes off. He sees the Sunglasses zeroing in on him. Jujube turns her back and walks away; she has her own life to get on with. No one else interferes; his fate is of little concern to others. The Sunglasses confiscate his ID, claiming it to be fake, and insist that, according to the information projected on their info-lenses, he is in fact a certain peasant with no right of residence in the city. "We've caught up with you, at last."

His denial is met with scorn. "You're what we call a Three-No. No ID. No residency permit. And… we forget what the third No refers to, but whatever it is you're supposed to have, you haven't got it."

Pine realises that Plum and Bamboo figured out he betrayed them, and are getting their revenge. He looks at the diners in the restaurant, all of them pretending they're unaware what's going on. What terrible actors they are! How grotesque they appear: the postures they arrange themselves in, the gestures they make, the faces they pull as they eat and chatter in a parody of normality. Desperately Pine grabs his phone. Sorry! You are in the bottom percentile of handsomeness! He views a version of himself – uglier than ever, blotched, wrinkled, hunched, and muttering how the System has confused him with someone altogether different – being led away.

Jonathan Tel is a novelist and short-story writer. He has won Sunday Times and Commonwealth short-story prizes

Index around the world

`INDEX NEWS`

47(02): 103/105 | DOI: 10.1177/0306422018784439

Danyaal Yasin looks at the threats to media freedom in Turkey, and other work Index has carried out in the past three months

IN THE FOUR years since Index launched Mapping Media Freedom, the platform used to monitor media freedom violations across 43 countries, there have been 618 reports of incidents in Turkey. At the time of writing, 368 attacks on journalists, from job losses to imprisonments, have been reported since the failed coup attempt in July 2016.

Sean Gallagher, Index's head of content, said: "The unprecedented crackdown on freedom of expression and journalism in Turkey underlined how fragile democracy and the rule of law are. The fact that President Erdogan himself was arrested for reading a poem should mean that he is a defender of freedom of expression, not one who attacks it." When he was mayor of Istanbul in 1997, Recep Tayyip Erdogan read out a poem that upset the then government and he was imprisoned on a charge of inciting religious hatred.

Twenty-nine Turkish journalists were jailed on terrorism charges in the last week of April alone, according to a United Nations statement. In May Erdogan visited the UK as part of a three-day trip to demonstrate the UK's "strong relationship" with Turkey, during which he met both Prime Minister Theresa May and the Queen.

On the day of his arrival, Index joined IFEX, English PEN and Reporters Without Borders outside Downing Street to call →

ABOVE: Index on Censorship took part in a protest in London this May to speak out for a free Turkish media during Turkish President Erdogan's visit to the UK capital

ABOVE: Index on Censorship magazine editor Rachael Jolley delivers a speech at the protest against Erdogan's crackdown on free expression, May 2018

→ for the release of imprisoned journalists and an end to Erdogan's crackdown on free speech. Hundreds of demonstrators spoke out for a free Turkish media, which has seen unprecedented attacks since the failed coup.

Speaking at the protest, Index on Censorship magazine editor Rachael Jolley said: "If Theresa May cares about free speech, if this government cares about free speech and free expression, this should be on the table for this meeting with President Erdogan.

"This [British] government often talks about its commitment to free speech, so let's see a sign of this in its international politics. How can we believe in a government's commitment to free expression if it is willing to meet international leaders where free expression is massively threatened and they do not talk about that?"

Protesters chanted "free Turkey media", voicing their disapproval of the current government. One Turkish demonstrator, who wished to remain anonymous, told Index: "It is so sad to see that my country is such a corrupt place that I can't even protest in a normal manner. I have to cover my face, because there are no rights in Turkey, there's no freedom.

"It's time to say stop, it's time to take action. There has to be something done about Erdogan imprisoning people for no reason – it's just not right."

The president's visit came during the campaign for the snap presidential and parliamentary election due to take place in Turkey on 24 June, nearly 18 months earlier than expected.

In a statement, Zeid Ra'ad Al Hussein, UN High Commissioner for Human Rights, said: "It is difficult to imagine how credible elections can be held in an environment where dissenting views and challenges to the ruling party are penalised so severely.

"The heavy police presence and arrests during the May Day protests also demonstrated yet again the severely limited space for freedom of peaceful assembly in the country."

May Day, also known as International Workers Day, saw tensions rise in Turkey, with more than 80 demonstrators arrested for marching on Taksim Square in Istanbul. Police declared the city's historic square off-limits because of security concerns, but small groups managed to break through. The square is symbolic for the workers' movement after 34 people were killed in 1977 during a May Day demonstration.

Protests erupted across the globe on 1 May this year, with workers and activists rallying against labour issues in their countries. Protesters in the Philippines expressed their frustrations with President Rodrigo Duterte, calling on him to end short-term employment in the country, something he promised to do on his campaign trail in 2016.

In France, hundreds marched across the capital against President Emmanuel Macron, who plans to end some worker protections as part of his pro-business reforms.

The day also saw thousands march in Spain, Greece, Germany and Cuba, against various inequalities.

May also saw journalists around the world continue to face attacks for their work, with World Press Freedom Day (on 3 May) highlighting the need to support those under fire.

Ten media workers were killed in two separate incidents in Afghanistan, with journalists among those who lost their lives in a suicide bomb attack in Kabul, which claimed 26 lives. Later the same day, BBC reporter Ahmad Shah was murdered in the Khost region.

The White House called the attacks "a senseless and heinous act", and many will welcome this condemnation, but this should not divert attention from media freedom violations in the USA. A report based on the findings of a mission to the country in January, which included Index on Censorship, found that press freedom continued to decline there.

Arrests, border stops, searches of devices, prosecution of whistleblowers and restrictions on the release of public information have all affected the ability of journalists to do their jobs. Co-authored by organisations including Article 19, CPJ and IFEX, the report showed that while current President Donald Trump's attacks on "fake news" outlets has led to a hostile climate for the press, press freedom violations also "rocketed under the Obama administration".

Index CEO Jodie Ginsberg said: "Animosity toward the press is undermining the public's right to information," adding that "the pressures that journalists are facing in the US are reflective of the toxic atmosphere towards journalism being stoked by global leaders".

In April, Index celebrated the 2018 Freedom of Expression Awards at a ceremony held at the Mayfair Hotel, in London. Wendy Funes, Habari RDC, the Egyptian Commission for Rights and Freedoms and The Museum of Dissidence won the awards for their work in journalism, digital activism, campaigning and arts, respectively. Recognised for their impact in their fields, the 2018 fellows visited the Index offices in

London for a week of dedicated training and support. Recently appointed Index advocacy and fellowships officer Perla Hinojosa said: "It was a humbling experience working with the fellows. Knowing what they go through on a day-to-day basis to defend the freedom of expression and seeing them get the recognition they deserve was the epitome of why the fellowship awards exist. It helps them in their work because they get exposure and international recognition for important work that sometimes goes unseen."

The awards are aimed at helping free expression across the globe and promoting those in need of support. One of this year's campaigning nominees, Open Stadiums, a group of Iranian women fighting against the restrictions on their use of public spaces, said just to be nominated "gave them strength",

There are no rights in Turkey, there's no freedom

adding: "If we get arrested, we know at least some people will know about our passion and the work we've done [over] the last 12 years. This campaign is our life's passion and now it's being recognised."

Wendy Funes, winner of the journalism award, also spoke of seeing the other people and groups nominated, telling Index: "Coming for the fellowship week was so enriching because it let us know, as fellows and nominees, that we're not the only ones going through the same types of issues.

"Seeing all the amazing people and groups let me know that we can come together and collaborate. We can help each other's stories be heard – not just in our own countries, but around the world." ⊗

Danyaal Yasin is the editorial assistant at Index on Censorship. He is also the Tim Hetherington/ Liverpool John Moores University 2018 fellow

Game on

47(02): 106/108 | DOI: 10.1177/0306422018784441

After the Parkland school shootings, Donald Trump decided video games, not guns, needed more controls in place, reports **Jemimah Steinfeld**

THE WORLD HEALTH Organization has just added gaming disorder to its list of mental health conditions. This May, in its 11th International Classification of Diseases, the WHO defined the disorder as a "persistent or recurrent" behaviour pattern of "sufficient severity to result in significant impairment in personal, family, social, educational, occupational or other important areas of functioning".

The move is likely to be cited by those who want to censor video games for other reasons. US President Donald Trump, for one. Just this March, Trump hosted a sudden meeting with representatives of the video games industry to talk about violence in video games. In addition to industry insiders, the meeting was attended by a host of prominent outspoken critics of video games, including Dave Grossman, who described first-person shooter games as "murder simulators" and said that, in the future, experts who denied links between video games and youth violence would "be viewed as the moral equivalent of Holocaust deniers".

Trump argued for more restrictions to prevent children from seeing or playing violent games.

The link between games and violence is hard to prove; less so is the link between games and politics. Trump's roundtable was a last-minute initiative occurring in the wake of the Parkland school shooting in Florida, when pressure was high for Trump to discuss gun control. Instead, he chose gaming – perhaps an easier target.

In a statement following the meeting, the Entertainment Software Association said: "We discussed the numerous scientific studies establishing that there is no connection between video games and violence, First Amendment protection of video games, and how our industry's rating system effectively helps parents make informed entertainment choices."

This is not the first time video game critics and advocates of First Amendment rights have collided. In 2011, in Brown v Entertainment Merchants Association, the US Supreme Court ruled that a California law restricting the sale of violent video games to minors was unconstitutional. Video games were protected speech under the First Amendment, like other forms of media, the court said.

Justice Antonin Scalia, writing the majority opinion in that 7-2 decision, dismissed the California argument that violent video games were linked to aggression in children, pointing out that the expert who provided that evidence admitted there were similar effects discovered in children who watched Bugs Bunny cartoons.

"The links between video games and violence, as with any cultural artefacts, are extremely ambiguous," said Sarah Ditum, a UK journalist with a background in gaming,

who writes about both the industry and politics. Ditum believes that the gaming industry is singled out more than other media and is "subject to scaremongering", although she said this wasn't anything new.

"Around the time of Columbine [the US high school shooting in 1999], gaming was still a pursuit that hadn't been engaged in by the kind of people engaged in public discourse and talking about things, whereas now I think most journalists have first-hand experience of games, even if they don't have a console themselves. So there is a bit less room for scaremongering than there used to be."

Just after the first computer emerged, so did video games. Early games included Noughts and Crosses and William Higinbotham's Tennis for Two in 1958. In the 1960s came one of the most groundbreaking games, Spacewar. At this stage, games were all played on computers and, therefore, the reserve of just a few. The 1970s saw them move from the sidelines to the mainstream, with games played on television sets. The biggest breakthrough came in 1985 with the release of the Nintendo Entertainment System. Since then, video gaming's popularity has only grown. Today, 65% of US households contain someone who plays video games regularly, according to the ESA.

Whilst their popularity has grown, so too have their detractors, leading to the introduction of a games ratings system in the USA in 1994.

Pressure was high for Trump to discuss gun control. Instead, he chose gaming

Australia introduced its own ratings systems at the same time, provoked by a moral panic over the game Night Trap, and has continued to operate one of the stricter policies. Until 2013, games had to pass higher standards than other media, allowing only those suitable for 15 years and below to be sold.

Despite the contested links between violence and video games, the idea that they provoke violence has been hard to shift →

→ – and continues to provoke calls for bans. At the end of March, parents of children at a primary school in London received text messages warning against the current hit game, Fortnite. "It is unsuitable for primary pupils and needs to be banned at home," it read.

In Germany, the relationship between gaming and politics is evident in the game Wolfenstein II: The New Colossus, an alternative-reality game in which Adolf Hitler won the war. The game's creators were made to shave off the former German leader's signature moustache in order to comply with the country's anti-Nazi laws.

Nowhere is the link more obvious, though, than in Uzbekistan, which banned 34 games last year, including harmless classics such as The Sims. Authorities said the games could be "used to propagate violence,

Today, 65% of US households contain someone who plays video games regularly

pornography, threaten security and social and political stability", as well as disturbing "inter-ethnic and inter-religious harmony". They could also distribute "false information about Uzbekistan and the distortion of its historic, cultural and spiritual values".

"They want to cultivate patriotism in the youth, yet the ban will only make things worse," said a social media user named Danilakhaidarov in the ban's wake.

Censorship of games has a major impact on what gets made and marketed. China, the world's largest video games market, has ramped up control in recent years in line with a general increase in censorship, introducing a series of new regulations.

They are "part of a bigger movement to take control of the internet", said Iain Garner, who works for Another Indie, a video game producer working in China.

All games must comply with various rules. Violence, sex and drugs are banned, "but it's also anything that contains any kind of political messaging or anything that is perceived to be immoral", Garner told Index.

The process of getting a game out in China can be long and tenuous. Garner says he worked on a game with a thief character in it "and we couldn't have a thief be a heroic protagonist because thieves are bad, so we ended up having to change the thief to a jester". Things that are the colour of blood can become a problem, he said, so the colour of a menu had to be changed in one instance.

What these hurdles have essentially done is not just drown out any alternative – and potentially political – voices in gaming; they have drowned out many smaller games companies. "Effectively, China killed its own indie game industry," said Garner.

"Games don't have a super-good profile politically at the moment as they stand, which I think is a shame as games also do incredibly ambitious, interesting things," said Ditum. She spoke of BioShock, which incorporates ideas by 20th-century dystopian and utopian thinkers such as George Orwell, Ayn Rand and Aldous Huxley.

In an interview in Index from 2014, Mia Bennett, a games publisher working between the UK and Iran, similarly said: "Some issues are easily disguised in games – women in action, historical points of view, free will – and it is great that gamers can play around with these ideas."

Yet Ditum does believe some monitoring of the industry is reasonable.

"There's a whole branch of gaming that is essentially underage pornography. It kind of passes under the radar because it belongs to games," she said.

"This is where you reach the negotiation point between freedom of expression and where the state should draw the line." ⊗

Jemimah Steinfeld is the deputy editor of Index on Censorship magazine